Reviews of Story Bridge

Simply put, the Story Bridge methodology, as presented in *Story Bridge: From Alienation to Community Action,* is, without question, the most powerful tool for community exploration and discovery I've seen in my 40 years of service in the storytelling renaissance. By tapping into our narrative assets, the Story Bridge process becomes a catalyst for unearthing our community values, our community challenges, and our vision of our community's future and, most important of all, the wisdom to forge a path of action to realize the community we desire.

-Jimmy Neil Smith, Founder and President Emeritus, International Storytelling Center

Story Bridge shares a deep truth: the fundamental assets of any community are the stories by which the people know themselves. Through clear and intuitive steps, *Story Bridge* carries the reader on a journey of group evolution and transformation, supported by the stories all around us in our organizations, companies, and communities. I've known Richard and Jules for most of two decades, and no one does more with the chaos of community. Mine and my family's stories have been part of their amazing process of asset based community development. I'm thrilled to see it in print in *Story Bridge.*

-John P. (Jody) Kretzman, Internationally recognized developer of Asset Based Community Development, and author of *Building Communities from the Inside Out: A Path Toward Finding and Mobilizing a Community's Assets*

As humans we all know community when we see, or more accurately, feel it. Building relationships and creating that sense of community has long been a primary goal of senior living, from independent living to memory care; yet until now, no one has been able to articulate a step by step process to achieve that goal. This concise and deeply wise book details how CPI has used life stories and the Story Bridge process time after time to activate "community" and empower individuals with diverse abilities and needs to create culture change. I think it's exactly what we've been looking for!

There's a deeply intuitive intelligence that lives in community and I believe accessing our individual and collective brilliance through community is the reason we're alive. CPI's *Story Bridge* provides a richly challenging yet enjoyable path towards that achievement, and once you've crossed the bridge, your life will be forever changed.

In this astounding work, authors Geer and Corriere empower people in all walks of life to improve the quality of their lives and relationships through the ancient technology of storytelling. They offer a brilliant weaving of essential concepts, real-life stories, and inspirational revelations. This is a book for anyone who seeks to share greater closeness, caring, and intimacy with others. It provides a road map for transforming friendships, families, organizations, and communities.

Thoughts on a Dream
"Do you want to hear a story?" This is perhaps the oldest and most welcoming of invitations throughout human history. Richard, Jules and their Story Bridge learning community bring us into a twenty-year journey of honoring citizen's stories and co-creating

community performances for health, healing, change and transformation.

Exquisitely crafted from their lips to your eyes *Story Bridge: From Alienation to Community Action* offers a behind the scenes view into the power of story making turned into community performances. Sharing stories, living into the performance of stories opens the possibility for relationships to form and deepen in ways that can transform individuals and a community.

There is no doubt that we are at a threshold point in history. What we do together in small and large groups could determine our fate. Helping individuals reconnect to each other in ways that promote a spirit of "We" is essential. *Story Bridge* is a potent ally that helps people remember the possibilities present for stories to foster intimate connections.

Story Bridge ends with important questions, worthy of stating at the beginning. "What if human groups "wake up," and come to consciousness and attention when their members begin to share stories? What if the collective human organism is only able to speak through the mouths of its people, their stories, and their conversations? What if story and conversation, intentionally applied, multiply many fold human intelligence and compassion?"

Yes, tell me a story and I'll tell you a story. Together let's *awaken* and co-create a community story. A community story performed is an act of *initiation* - welcoming us back into a community that we can all call *home*.

When we achieve this life sustaining sense of community, we would indeed move from alienation to committed action crossing over the Story Bridge to a future the nurtures life for everyone and the planet.

This book is designed for anyone interested and committed to promoting life affirming individual and community change. Students and teachers alike from the fields of Theater, community organizing…..

-David G. Blumenkrantz, Ph.D., M.Ed.
The Center for the Advancement of Youth, Family & Community Services, Inc., Glastonbury, CT 2012

...I watched the Story Bridge methodology engage and bond people of diverse backgrounds and perspectives. I believe this work is crucial to demonstrate the integral weaving of Storytelling as applied and performance art—an art that articulates, moves, and empowers communities.

-Joseph Sobol, PhD, Program Coordinator *ETSU Graduate Program in Storytelling,* author of *The Storytellers' Journey: An American Revival*

I love this book and I am, at this very moment, using your framework and structure ideas for my next residency with 5th graders. It is the piece of the puzzle that I have been looking for in my work and it feels as though it brings the work I have been doing for years full circle and into completeness.

As an international educator and teaching artist, I believe that Richard and Jules have tapped into a rich and vast natural resource that each of us possesses -- our stories. *Story Bridge* outlines the process of harvesting stories, bringing them into performance and then using these stories as a springboard for conversations and inspiration toward transformational change of individuals and their communities. It is my belief that the compelling model they share in this book is of great value to educational communities nationally and internationally.

I had the opportunity to attend the Staging Change Institute in the fall of 2011 with Richard, Jules, Juanita and David and this experience had a remarkable impact on my work with educators and with students. The Story Bridge process begins with attention to and creation of a safe place for participants. As the storyteller invites us into their story, the active role of listener enables us to transform from the mindset of "me" to "we" in a deep, thoughtful and meaningful way. As personal stories are shared, the "universal" nature of these stories becomes clear. And through the vast web of personal stories we learn about history, human nature, compassion and culture while we experience a myriad of emotions ranging from sadness, fear, laughter, anger, regret and joy. We are offered the opportunity to reflect upon the past, become active in the present and even have the chance to glimpse into the future. Imagine the positive impact this creative process could have in educational communities across the country! Thank you Richard and Jules for sharing this profound creative work with us, we can change the world, one story at a time!

> -Mary Knysh, Rhythmic Connections: international educator and teaching artist, author of *"Innovative Drum Circles: from Rhythm to Melody and Beyond"*, *"BoomDoPa"- a Facilitator's Guide to Ethnic Influenced Music Improvisation,"* and *"Drumming and Storytelling"* DVD

I have witnessed the transforming outcomes that Geer and Corriere have produced through leading community storytelling events. *Story Bridge* is about that remarkable process that leads communities out of the various dead ends that problem focused thinking often leads to. You will discover how the Story Bridge leads us from individualism to community – from intervention to collaboration, and from mixed results to sustainable initiatives that are truly good for all. As a researcher on sustainable urban planning and a consultant for churches on community mission, it is my opinion that *Story Bridge* is a must-have-resource for practitioners that are concerned with the transformational path that gets us to good together.

> -Ron Pate, PhD, Author of *Narrative Processes in Urban Planning*, Director of GOOD SO$_2$LUTIONS, a clean air initiative in Portland, OR

Community Performance Press
www.CommunityPerformanceInternational.com

Producer: Melissa Block

Editors: Juanita Brown, Jules Corriere, Frankie Wolff

Cover Design: Ricki St. John

Photos: Richard Owen Geer and Katy Rosolowski

Book Design and Typesetting: Melissa Block

ISBN-13: 978-1480101814

ISBN-10: 1480101818

Printed in the United States of America

Story Bridge

From Alienation to Community Action

Errar)
I look forward to sharing the journey with such a colleague as you as we build the bridges at SMC,
Richard 10/13

Richard Owen Geer and Jules Corriere

Illustrated by Nancy Sylvia

with
Melissa Block, Juanita Brown, David Isaacs

and the learning community
of the Jonesborough Yarn Exchange

ACKNOWLEDGEMENTS

Thousands of extraordinary people on three continents have contributed to these ideas. All of you are in our hearts.

Adrienne St. John
Ashley Cooper
Attendees at the first Staging Change Institute
Barbara Carder and the People of Scrap Mettle SOUL
Ben Barge
Bill Grow and the Swamp Gravy Institute
Bob Browning
Brackley Frayer
Brett McCluskey
Camille Sullivan
Catherine Jordan
Charlotte Phillips
Curtis Holsopple
David Blumenkrantz
Dena Adriance
Derek Davidson
Ed Wolff
Elizabeth Foster-Shaner
Frankie Wolff
Gayle Grimsley
Heather McCluskey
Ingrid Christiansen
Jack Travis
Janna Browning
Jason Bolen
Jimmy Neil Smith
Jo Carson
Jody Kretzman
Joey Fargar
John David and Esther Mable Yoder and the people of Pieced Together
Joseph A. Varga
Joseph Sobol
Joy Jinks and Karen Kimbrel and the people of Swamp Gravy
Julie Christiansen
Justin Carbonella
Kay van Norman
Keresey Proctor
Kevin Iega Jeff
Khristine Rogers
Linda Burnham
Margaret Ashmore
Marion and Anita Way and the People of Institut Central Do Povo
Mary Kynsh
Maxine Roby

Naomi Davis
Penny Cook
Phyllis Fabozi
Rachael Allison and the People of Folk Salad
Robert Gipe
Roberta Rosenberg and Terry Lee
Ron Pate
Rose McGee
Scott Miller
Steve Durland
Susana Bloch
The People of Bethel New Life
The People of Boogaloo Broadcasting Company
The People of Celery Soup
The People of City Bridges
The People of Grit and Grace
The People of HillFire
The People of Just Home in the Mountains
The People of Land of Spirit
The People of Pot Luck in the Muck
The People of Salkehatchie Stew
Virginia Hubbell
Wes Sullivan

CONTENTS

THE STORY BRIDGE HELPS A COMMUNITY
(ORGANIZATION, CORPORATION) MOVE FROM
BEING A COLLECTION OF ALIENATED INDIVIDUALS
TO A COHESIVE FORCE FOR COMMITTED ACTION.
THROUGH THIS GROUP PROCESS, PEOPLE MOVE
FROM A FOCUS ON "I" TO A FOCUS ON "WE." THEY
ARE DRAWN BY THE OPPORTUNITY TO SHARE
PERSONAL STORIES, AND HEAR THE SAME FROM
NEIGHBORS AND COLLEAGUES. THROUGH THE FUN
AND THE WORK OF SHARING STORIES, STRANGERS
BECOME FAMILY. ATTACHMENT, RELATIONSHIP,
AND COMMITMENT GROW BETWEEN PEOPLE WHO
CROSS THE BRIDGE TOGETHER TO A NEW VISION
OF THEIR PLACE.

INTRODUCTION

In the 1960s, theater for social change consisted of performances against injustice. Playwrights, directors, and actors staged the stories of oppressed others. And, most of the time, that's as far as it went. A decade later, when Richard first noticed the power of performance to build community among his casts, he didn't realize he was in the vanguard of a new kind of socially active theater. This new form moved performance toward participation—people are affected more by what they experience, than by what they observe. When he directed a play, he noticed two important outcomes: first, the play, and, second, the community the players became. This very special sort of theater community is called "ensemble." Generous, creative, playful, and spontaneous, an ensemble of actors love each other, their audience, the theater, and the act of creating together. A question arose that would eventually direct both the lives of both Richard Geer and Jules Corriere.

> *"What if a rehearsal room was as big as a community? What sort of a community could that become?"*

Forty years later, the Story Bridge process is a partial answer. The larger question might be, "How do humans form communities that benefit everyone. How do we get to "good?"

In practical terms, the story-to-change process can make significantly less stressful the ticklish job of meeting new people, learning about their lives and needs, and building with them in the shared space of community. The Bridge moves people from "I" to "We," through a currency in which we're all rich—life experience expressed as personal stories.

The Story Bridge is a sequence of fun, easily engaged activities that help strangers become friends, and help friends improve the place they share. When the process is most successful, it tips over into a new paradigm, and brings people into relationship beyond roles, and agendas, even beyond words. Solutions replace problems. Service and caring become a privilege.

During our twenty years of practicing Community Performance, the structure of this bridge to community has become ever more clear. Once upon a time, we thought exchanging and performing stories was enough. The act of sharing our own stories and witnessing those of others did begin a shift. But there was not enough supporting that shift, and, gradually, the positive changes reverted to the *status quo*. But year after year, working in communities from Colorado to Chicago to Rio, new practices evolved. With the incorporation of World Café conversation, the bridge stood firm. The story-to-change process, spanned the chasm from strangers to change makers.

Is it "finished"? Of course not. Everyone who crosses the bridge is a pioneer. Each with a view to what is possible next. But whatever that "next" is, the bridge, as always, starts with story.

Story Bridge 4

ON THE NEAR SHORE, THE ANCHORAGE OF THE BRIDGE, ITS ON-RAMP, IS STORIES, LOCAL, PERSONAL STORIES OF THE HEART. SHARING HEART STORIES DRAWS PEOPLE OUT OF THEMSELVES TO BEGIN THE JOURNEY. WE NEVER FORGET WHEN LIFE TRULY CHALLENGES US—THE MORNING WE GOT THE DIAGNOSIS, THE DAY MY FIRST CHILD WAS BORN, THE LOSS OF OUR WAY OF LIFE. AT LIFE'S TURNING POINTS, WE LAY UP STORES OF HARD-EARNED WISDOM, IN THE FORM OF STORIES. WE ARE WILLING TO SHARE THESE STORIES WHEN WE FEEL SAFE AND TRULY LISTENED TO—WITNESSED. TO WITNESS IS TO BRING OUR FULL SELVES—HEART, MIND, SPIRIT, BREATH, AND BODY—TO THE ACT OF LISTENING. THE GRAVITATIONAL FIELD OF WITNESSING PULLS EVENTS INTO THE SACRED SHAPE OF STORY. THE FEELING OF WITNESS IS REVERENCE.

CHAPTER ONE: STORY

A community is an organism. It is constantly processing and adapting to new information. A central aspect of any organism is self-regulation. One of the ways a community self-regulates is through its stories. Stories surface issues that need to be aired. Stories move important material into the realm of its citizens' discourse where it can be considered and acted on. Of key importance to the understanding of any community are the stories that surface at a given moment. The stories that simply "come up" reveal hidden insights. The Story Bridge operates on this truth: community is constantly in conversation with itself through its stories.

When we gather stories from individuals, we gather with the assumption that the story is true individually and communally. In Union, South Carolina, we attended our first interview, and asked the question, "Tell me something you want people to know about you." We heard a single story about good parenting. When we went to other interviews and story circles, we heard more stories about parenting, good parenting, good grand-parenting. What we discovered transcended any one story—we were listening in on the community's grief and hope.

Union was the town where, eight years previously, Susan Smith, a white woman, had drowned her two children and then gone on national television to claim they'd been car-jacked by a black man. Days later, with the nation holding its breath, she confessed. Oprah, Geraldo, CNN, and all of the news networks descended upon Union during the trial, and all year, Union and her citizens were held under scrutiny for

Smith's actions. The media labeled Union as "The home of the world's worst mother," and for eight years, the community lived under that scarlet phrase.

When we heard one story about good parenting, we put it in the general folder of stories. When we got a second and a third and fourth similar story, we knew we'd found something on which the community was spending a lot of psychic energy. Unconsciously, folks were defending their town and their families. Their stories of good parenting countered what was being said about them on television and in the news. "We are good people who care about our children." Among these stories, we also heard a very difficult story that would serve as an historical parallel to the Susan Smith story, which we'd been asked not to tell.

We spoke to the core team about the theme that was emerging. They were excited by it and wanted to use it. The result was a play about a young man trying to forgive his cruel mother; surrounding it were stories of wonderful parenting. The local audience experienced a catharsis when the young man forgave his mother, and redemption through the many stories of children, well loved and well raised. *American Theatre* said, "*Turn the Washpot Down* may not save Union's life, but it has already saved its soul." (Burnham, 2003)

In the play, *Turn the Washpot Down,* each teller told *her* truth, and *her community's* truth as well. For over twenty years, in community performance plays written in towns across the country, that truth has held. The collected stories of individuals hold within them the hopes, fears, and struggles of the whole community. We witnessed the self-regulation of a community through its stories.

The community voice speaks through the peoples' stories.

Stories that rise through individuals into the shared space carry power to heal teller and community. Two kinds of stories bring about this healing. Proleptic stories come from the past but point to the future—if it has happened before, then it can happen again. Proleptic stories bring hope to a community that whatever they are struggling with now can be met, because it has been met before.

A Holographic story carries the community's circumstance in its narrative, as the shard of a broken holographic plate carries the entire image. We discovered one such story in Colquitt, Georgia, between a young African American man and the town's white fire chief. Their story pointed to the place that energy was frozen in the community, and where the thawing, healing, change might begin.

Shadow and the Fire Chief

The two outstanding volunteer organizations in the tiny town of Colquitt (pop. 2000) are immediately across the street from one another. When Swamp Gravy, the original Community Performance project, began performing in Cotton Hall, there were no bathrooms, so patrons had to cross Main, the town's busiest street, to use the restrooms in the Colquitt/Miller Fire Department.

The firemen volunteered as crossing guards. That's how little Emanuel got to know them, as they helped people safely cross to and from the show. More than bodily necessity drove Emanuel to the station. He put up with being in Swamp Gravy because his mother and brother loved it, but Emanuel's heart was with the shiny engines and the larger-than-life firemen who rode them, roaring to the fires.

Firemen performed in the stories of Swamp Gravy, and Swamp Gravy told the stories of firemen. When an alarm came in during a performance, things could get crazy, as half the men in the cast rushed out the door.

Emanuel Haire was five when his mother, Veronica, brought him into Swamp Gravy. At thirteen Emanuel began showing up at the firehouse even when Swamp Gravy wasn't running. "You don't train a fireman with a hose; you train him with a broom," said Chief Tully. And on any day you could see the men doing just that, cleaning, polishing and sweeping—all the white men and one black kid.

Chief Craig Tully was worried. His department was losing its edge. He'd started with less than nothing, twenty years before. Often, in the early days, the first fire he had to put out was the fire engine itself, which could burst into flames as it labored to a call. But Tully was a disciplinarian and a charismatic leader. He took the community's need for a good fire department to the people and they responded. His boot drives were legendary and frequent. When a fireman walked up to your car, boot in hand, the obligation as a citizen was to put money in that boot. Boot by boot, Tully and his men built the best volunteer department in the state of Georgia.

Tully didn't start out as a fan of Swamp Gravy. He wanted nothing to do with "that mess" across the street. But his job was public safety. Every performance his men escorted actors and audience from the parking lot to the theater, and then stood by should there be a need for first aid. Little Emanuel often stood with them. One night a patron fell and injured himself, and Tully quickly came to his aid. It was the first time he'd set foot inside the theater during a performance. The patron, badly enough hurt to need medical attention, but stable, begged Tully not to disturb the performance by bringing in a gurney till after the show. So Tully sat through the second act of his first Swamp Gravy performance. That was in the late 90s. And when we interviewed Craig seven years later, he hadn't missed a show. We don't mean he hadn't missed a *season;* he hadn't missed a single *performance.*

The first generation fire fighters had to do everything, fight fires, wash trucks, and hold bake sales. The fireman's whole family was involved, and the sense of mission was palpable in the all-white force. In the early years, there wasn't enough money. They needed extrication equipment, for instance, but the price tag was simply out of reach. So they made do, jury-rigged solutions, and managed to save lives and property with nothing but the will to do so.

Then came the wreck they would never forget. The man's injuries weren't immediately fatal; a quick trip to the ER could have saved him, but he was pinned in the wreckage. He was conscious, and they held his hand, read him the Bible, kept his spirits up, and raced the clock with hack saws, pry bars, winches, and every bit of might. But he died, bled out. Nothing they could do was enough. The next day Tully and the men showed up at the bank to sign papers personally guaranteeing the loan for the Jaws of Life, the tool which could have saved the man's life.

The department's motto is "When called, we respond." And they'd built their reputation on the quickest response to every call. What gets a fireman's blood pumping is a big house fire or a multi-car crash. But the bread and butter calls are grass fires, abandoned sheds, and fender benders. This is what had Chief Tully worried. After a while some volunteers began to pick and choose their calls. When the walkie talkies announced a grass fire on the far side of town, some firemen just didn't respond. That kind of thing happened over and over. That's when the relationship between the white fire chief and the black Swamp Gravy teen began to exert its pull. From *Nuthin But a Will*, Jules Corriere's play for Swamp Gravy:

> TULLY: *The fire department had been around for a while. We had trucks, station houses, and our own shirts. We'd strut in those shirts, boy. I'm almost ashamed to say, but we got kind of to the point where we thought we were a little better than we really were. We'd been this homegrown family thing, then we sorta got our stuff together, and some of the family thing went away. Then, out of nowhere, these kids show up. Shadow was first. No matter where I turned, there he was. I couldn't throw a bucket of water behind me without him getting wet. Before long, he's got friends coming, riding their bikes. They wanted to serve. Did whatever it took. I didn't know what to do at first, group of young kids, didn't think they'd last, so we tested them. Had them clean, wash trucks, come to meetings on time. They did. They were business. There'd be a call, and they'd all come across right down here by the liquor store to get to the station. They couldn't afford a car, didn't have a car between 'em, and most of the time, they were the first ones here on their bikes, and they came to every call. We'd got to the point we were picking our calls, but these boys on the bicycle brigade came to every one. That was the turning point of this fire*

department. We was going through a struggle, and these boys showed us what we forgot. They cared enough to do whatever it took to get here. Reminded us why we started the department. When called, we respond. We don't pick and choose. That's what brought the fire department back, them fellows on that bicycle brigade.

The racial integration of the department didn't come about through a court injunction or a protest, it happened because of the relationship of two people. When thirteen year-old Emanuel came across the street from Swamp Gravy, he came to do his part, just as he'd done with the integrated cast of Swamp Gravy. Trouble was, there was no role for him. But he didn't go away. He swamped toilets, he swept floors, he rode with the men to the fires, he knocked the kinks out of the hose. When his grades fell, he didn't ride. Craig made him sweep and swamp just the same until the grades came up. Craig was tough, but Emanuel was tougher. He was always there. Craig came to calling him "Shadow" because he was always right there, right behind the chief. "I took him in like he was mine," Craig said.

Later it was car loans and college applications that Craig helped out with. But Emanuel earned all of it, and he wasn't alone. His friends noticed what he was up to, and pretty soon there was a brigade of black youth, too young and too poor to drive, but called by the thrill, and determined to serve. You'd know there was a fire, not because the trucks were gone, or the lot was full of pickups; you'd know it first because there was a pile of bikes on the front lawn. In the race to the firehouse, boys with bikes beat men with cars. The boys taught the men what commitment was. Craig learned from Shadow. He found what was lost, and he and Emanuel, together, brought it back to the firehouse.

To reach into the mind and heart of a community, asking it to reveal itself, we often begin individual interviews or story circles with a neutral prompt, "Tell about a time when your life changed..." With a neutral prompt the storyteller can go anywhere story beckons.

In Jonesborough, Tennessee, we heard the voices of community story proclaiming it to be a very special sort of home. Besides several over-the-top stories of how beautifully the community cared for its families, and dozens more filled with specifics of love and involvement, there were also stories of people who were excluded. One was the story of segregated schools. Another was about a shunning and the refusal of the shunned family to leave Jonesborough. And finally, a story about a migrant worker whose angry neighbors screamed at her to go home, and the realization, by this Latino woman, that, despite the hatred, she was home. Her answer became the play's title, *I Am Home*.

A neutral prompt brought forth the story of Emanuel and Craig, too. We were visiting with friends, just catching up with Colquitt after a five year absence. We tugged on a thread. Our interest triggered a memory and an amazing story emerged. A vision for racial harmony and high performance community is contained in Emanuel and Craig's holographic story, which might be interpreted this way:

> *The energy of the African Americans in Colquitt is bottled up, and the full energy of the whole community, white and black, is stopped until whites and blacks liberate it. Not through confrontation or conflict, but through the shared love of place, work and each other, the old ways give way. The result is*

a better community and proof that diversity creates excellence.

Colquitt's story instructs Colquitt where to look for reserves of energy for change and success in these hard times.

Connecting Through Our Stories

Since time out of mind, the story arts have been compared to the fabric arts—spinning, sewing, knitting, weaving, and quilting. After listening to hundreds of life stories, an image rose up of what transpires in the sacred space of telling and listening.

> *Imagine story itself, made visible as it is told. Out of the teller's heart floats a silken cord the shape and color of her story. As she concludes, one end anchors in her heart, the other in heart of the witness. Then roles reverse. The witness becomes the teller, soon his story lies beside, paralleling, overlapping, entwined with, hers, the similar shapes and colors of the stories touching, shining together. Anchored in each other's hearts, the story cords become the bridge over which each travels in understanding to the other. This is the beginning of change.*

Twenty years ago, we thought these threads might be the bridge entire. But a few threads are not strong enough to support sustained change. Nevertheless, this vision of heart sharing carries a lot of truth: Story is the basic building material and the way onto the bridge. Story creates the relationships and connections necessary to sustain and support growth.

For story to come forth, a hospitable and safe place must be made where all can sit in equality. Later, as folks grow in the process, they realize they are bound by their common humanity, the recognition that all people hope and all suffer. But in the beginning, small things, like a well-formed circle of chairs, friendly faces, presence, vulnerability, and authentic facilitation, set the stage. Something larger than you or me does the rest. It is something with which we participate but over which we do not have control. Within it, we are not individuals, but parts of its larger self. The community we define by our presence begins, one heart at a time, to re-define us.

As the process of story sharing goes forward, individual agency shifts to the agency of participation, which is different in every way. "I" becomes "we." When stories are reverently shared, one on one, or in a circle, we feel love for the other persons. Judgment is vacated; we are drawn inside the speakers' points of view, and, with them, experience the worlds of their stories.

If we choose to go with a teller into her story, we will follow her down the passages of her choosing, along her thread, into her labyrinth. Together we'll find the way out. We are her witnesses. She takes the journey for herself and us. Our reverent listening empowers her daring, helping her go deep. And our presence helps her to find her way back out, too. This reciprocal act creates a profound result: relationship between teller and listener, connection between the members of the group. And insight, by everyone, into the mystery of the story. We feel the mystery and the story. As we start across the bridge, we feel the upwelling power of "We."

Story as an Act of Liberation: NiNi Reclaimed

Story calls forth story. One by one, as we draw stories out of each other, the world we share appears. To humans, stories are the world. This is not a metaphor. Everything we know is spun into and out of being through stories. The power of gods spinning universes into being is the power of story. The fragility of you in this brief brutish life of yours, or the greatness of you in this fabulous, long, and lovely adventure, is story, all story.

Little NiNi lived alone in a dark room to which her older, adult self, Sonia, held the only key. Sonia feared little NiNi for the terrible things the child knew, yet agreed to take us to visit her in her story. For three hours we journeyed into NiNi's world where rape and molestation by three generations of her male relatives devastated her young life. And then we journeyed out, led by NiNi, who at fourteen, all by herself, escaped her prison. As she closed her story, Sonia said:

> I've told all this before, over years, to therapists. But I've never told it before in one sitting, as a story. I see something now. NiNi was all alone, had no power, and no one to defend her. Yet she survived in that terrible place and finally escaped from it. Today, as I told her story to you, I realized that NiNi is a survivor. More than that, I realized that NiNi is a hero.

Sonia no longer hated and feared little NiNi, no longer needed to keep her locked in that dark room of shame.

We witnessed Sonia's story, that's all. Story sharing is healing, but it is not therapy. This is important. No one is out to fix anyone. We are only to accompany, reverently listening, as one person journeys into her story in our presence. In that act, marvels are discovered by all, and the result is relationship.

Although the story was entirely hers, witnessing exerted a centripetal force on Sonia. Witnessing helped Sonia pull her story into a circle instead of a series of events. The circle brings closure and awakening. The teller knows her story must end—it isn't a therapy session that will pick up again later. Something deep draws her and her listeners to the conclusion. It is not always a happy ending, but it is an ending, a place where we land, together, after the journey. The force of teller and witnesses overcame the story's apparent downward arc. Sonia took us from a beautiful room in her home overlooking a great still lake into the dark rooms of her childhood, *and back home again*. The power of teller and witness dedicating their energies to the *sharing of a story*, led to a reunion for NiNi and Sonia, and new relationships.

We made no comment about Sonia's story, only asked her for details to better understand. Yet together we increased each other's wellness. Something *whole*some happened for each of us. Integrity comes from the word "integer" and means one. Sonia and NiNi were integrated. Sonia, in sharing, became one with us, as well.

The process drew together two communities; the outside community that we and Sonia shared was strengthened by the bonds of our friendship. Inside herself, Sonia and NiNi—alienated characters in her interior community—came together, too. And though we never experienced such abuse, elements of Sonia's story were our story, too, and increased our wellness. Her story, like all good stories, nudged us to examine ourselves. Where might we be alienated from parts of ourselves?

We experience such a journey as a gift. One caveat. As we listen, we'll likely feel the tug to repay in the only possible currency, another story. We all know the feeling. As we hear another's story, a shift happens in the solar plexus, a feeling that means "I have a related story to share." As we listen to the other's story, a tension builds, becomes anticipation, narrows our focus, brings us forward in the chair, arouses us, and probably increases heart rate and blood pressure. As if in preparation for physical effort, we tense at the starting line of our story. Caution. When our urge to tell our own story begins to build, we must continue fully to attend to the story being told by the other. The magic of story sharing collapses if the room fills up with people who are no longer listening, but simply biding time until they can speak. To return yourself to the place of listening with reverence, jot a reminder note, and then turn your full attention back to listening.

Since those amazing three hours, we've remained friends and woven our stories into the larger community which holds us. Aliveness poured into us and made us thirsty for more aliveness. What remains—beyond the process of gathering stories for a sharing, a play, or a celebration—is relationship and community.

Circle, Spiral

Story often starts in one place, moves out into adventure, then brings us back to the place we began—but with a difference. The teller's journey is first. Through him we leave and return to normal life; in between is the artificial yet life-like world of his story. Second is the journey of the character(s). Their story often begins and ends in the same place; many stories are about leaving and returning home.

Other times the story begins and ends in different places, but with a sense of completion. Think of the immigrant leaving her home, traveling great distances, beginning an entirely new life—new place, new husband, family, language, and faith—and realizing at long last that this new and different place has somehow, mysteriously, become the place she left...home. Third, the witness' experience, like the teller's, departs from this moment and place and returns to it, changed, at the story's end.

> We shall not cease from exploration
> And the end of all our exploring
> Will be to arrive where we started
> And know the place for the first time.
> T.S. Eliot, from Little Gidding, lines 239-42

Story is about change. Nothing is quite the same after it. For the central characters this is invariably true. We depart on a night adventure with Peter Pan and finally come back to our own snug beds. But we carry forever the experience, and it has changed us. Wendy departs as a child, returns as a woman. Her body—the body of every pubescent girl—irrevocably changes as she falls bleeding to the earth of Neverland. After her night flight, her very cells are different.

This is a clue to story's power. Our very cells are changed when, like Wendy, we put ourselves in the path of a story, answer its challenge, and step out of its beckoning window to stand on air. Think of the narrative arc you remember from literature class. It takes off like an airliner with all of us on board and climbs through the turbulence of complicating incidents to soar above the clouds to its moment of truth, the dogfight to the death that is its climax, and then swoops in a swift and satisfying descent to land on solid earth.

But not the same earth. Here, the perspectives are different, the relationships are enriched, and our heart is full of regard, caring, and compassion for the people whose stories surround us. We have begun to cross the Bridge. The relationships that will carry us forward are forming. We are moving from "I" to "We."

THE FIRST PIER SUPPORTING THE BRIDGE IS PERFORMANCE.
PERFORMANCE, AT EVERY SCALE. IT CAN BE AS BIG AS A
FULL BLOWN ORIGINAL PLAY OF LOCAL STORIES WITH A CAST
OF ONE HUNDRED, OR AS SMALL AS ONE TELLING ANOTHER'S
STORY BACK IN THE FIRST PERSON. WITNESSING IS
PERFORMANCE, TOO: THE PERFORMANCE OF LISTENING
SHAPES THE TELLER'S STORY. PERFORMANCE IS ALWAYS
ROLE PLAYING, MOVING US OUT OF OURSELVES, AND
CHANGING OUR POINT OF VIEW. WE JOURNEY IN THE SKIN OF
ANOTHER TO PLACES WE'VE NEVER BEFORE KNOWN AND
UNDERSTANDINGS WE'VE NEVER HAD. PERFORMANCE SHIFTS
PERSPECTIVE—"MY WORLD" BECOMES "OUR WORLD." AND IT
CREATES THE ENERGY NECESSARY TO CROSS THE STORY
BRIDGE.

CHAPTER TWO: PERFORMANCE

Story and Performance, Inseparable

Performance, as it is commonly defined, only half explains what happens to and between people when stories are shared. We normally think of performance (theater, dance, platform storytelling) is something broadcast out to an audience. Reception by the audience is not part of the usual definition.

Sharing stories requires a definition of performance that is more *implementation* than just *presentation*. The word "perform" comes from the Old French and originally had this more specific implication. *Parfornir* means "to do, carry out, finish, accomplish."

A story is not done, carried out, accomplished until *both* teller and audience have performed it. The teller performs it when it is sent. The listener performs it when it is received. Only through the active engagement of both parties, can story/performance work its transformational magic.

But how can simply hearing a story be performance? To answer this, let's take a moment to look at what story is. Story is a profound human innovation. Mortals are slaves to time and space, but, through story, they master both. "Once upon a time, in a kingdom far away," proclaims story's special power. Through story, the teller leaves herself and embodies a cast of others in another place and time. While she cannot actually disappear into them, her impersonation can be so strong that the witnesses may feel she has. The little boy enthralled by monsters in a book can become too terrified by his daddy's growls. The storyteller is his daddy, but when he growls and talks in that voice, he is also the monster. The storyteller is not the character, but he is not, not the character. The monster winks out from daddy's eye, steals his voice, claws his hands, and too thoroughly (but thrillingly!) convinces his little listener.

In our definition of performance, a listener can do more than passively receive. When we listen with our full attention, the story comes alive *inside* us. The little boy feels the monster's claws. Or the long-dead wife, living again through her old husband's words, appears as a young bride in the listener's mind, *as the listener performs the story.*

When stories go to places of emotion, teller and witness step out of themselves to follow. This is how a listener is also a performer. As listeners are *moved* by story, they step out and into other times, places, events, and characters. When people share stories with one another, they also step into each other. There is mystery in this. Teller and listener merge.

After the story, after they have resumed themselves, this portal between them remains open. It can be re-inhabited with a word, even a look. Teller and witness have bonded. The story's intensity has opened both, making them members of a single family, neighbors in the same community of experience.

The transformational magic of story, shared between two or more humans, doesn't require a stage at all. Even shared in a whisper, it has the power to change lives. When shared among a group of people, it can change a whole community. Community by community, it can change the world. Margaret Mead's most famous utterance is a statement about a group of people who share one story in just this way:

> "*Never doubt that a small group of thoughtful, committed people can change the world. Indeed, it is the only thing that ever has.*"

Performing to Change

In Asheville, North Carolina, we worked with a company dedicated to providing services to the homeless population, with the intention of ending chronic homelessness. Their desire was to create a performance, not just of homeless and formerly homeless, but of the business leaders, students at nearby University of North Carolina at Asheville, and local residents. It would be an opportunity to bring people together who might never have met, and dispel some of the myths and misrepresentations of homeless people. In rehearsal, it was difficult to know who was homeless and who was homed.

The project enabled seventy people, aged five to eighty-six, to get to know each other, perform together, have fun, and importantly, not to be afraid of each other. Homeless people are often just as afraid as others are of them. The homeless never know if someone is going to see them and call the police, or cross the street, or look away and inflict the most painful experience—indifference. We all want to be seen, to be called by name. We all want to know that others see us and acknowledge that we exist and are important.

Stories collected for the play, *Always Expect Miracles*, dealt with people whose lives were either cherished or ignored, and the consequences of that attention or indifference. It also explored times when they may have looked away, ignoring that small voice asking them to go beyond their fears and prejudice.

During the process of rehearsing and performing, cast members looked to each other for insights into their characters. "When the shelter door was shut, how did you react?" Or, "What did you like about being homeless? What made you laugh?" Performing with each other, they moved deeper into each other. Gary, formerly homeless, a vet from the veteran's home, surprised everyone when he helped fellow actor, Carol, with her performance as a nurse. Gary had been a physician. Suppositions were shattered, and everyone, including us, the directors, had our assumptions turned upside down. Gary and Carol became best friends. The two of them have since travelled to several states to watch our Community Performances, and to witness the emergence of other friendships, like theirs. They talk to cast members, and encourage them to open up and get to know each other. You never know whom you might be performing with. Maybe your new best friend.

A paramount power of performance is to try out new possibilities. In Asheville, homeless cast members got to stand inside other stories, in which they could practice, safely, a new way of being. If you mess up, it is okay, you don't lose your role. Whereas, in real life, Marcus experienced the frustration of having employers "give him a chance," but look for him to make a mistake, because it was expected.

Performance is a gravity-free space, in which stumbles have reduced consequence. Giving yourself the freedom to make "big mistakes" is the surest route to success. In the rehearsal room, Marcus was encouraged to trust his intuition, to act on impulse. If he had trouble, there was a family of directors and actors there to help him succeed in his role. He kept succeeding. With each new success, he brought more of himself. He began to do more and more with the production; his confidence rose. He *performed himself into a new Marcus.* He worked with his fellow actors, who encouraged his performance, gave him attention and care, and the room to succeed or fail. He saw that other people—business leaders and teachers—also struggled to learn their lines and remember staging. Everyone was succeeding at some things and messing up in others, and they were all pitching in to pull everything together to create a group success. Marcus found himself included. He experienced himself as a resource for others, handling a role close to Marcus' own experience. Folks were eager for the things he had to share, and eager to share in return with Marcus. The experience led him to try on other roles, on stage and off.

Marcus came to everything. He was there with the technical team to move furniture and build sets. He was outside the building shoveling snow off the path because he knew 86 year old Eloise would be coming to rehearsal. He had recently applied for housing, and during our month of performance, those who had worked with Marcus gave glowing remarks about his reliability. These were people who could never have been references for Marcus, because they never would have known him, but for the project they shared. As they performed together, they came to trust and rely on each other. The weekend before we closed, Marcus went from homeless to homed. He had performed his way into a new life.

Performance demands interaction—the story must be told, it must be heard. Whether in a circle where teller shares with others who share their listening, or on a stage where each is by turns teller and listener, performance demands engagement. Shyness and fear will give way, because the situation of performance enables transformation. Performance (from listening through acting on stage) eases the process of meeting, engagement, and getting comfortable with others. Through performance, we learn to trust ourselves to step out and into the other. Without performance, none of these relationships, and none of these changes, would happen.

The Energy of Performance

When we perform we are beside ourselves. The combination of story and performance reveal the self to the self, breaking in on the flow of life to re-contextualize it. It might seem that story builds with words, and performance with action, but truly, neither can express without the other. There is no story without performance, or performance without story. Story locked in a book is not story; performance, locked in body, is not performance. Each is the emancipation of the other.

Why do we express stories? Ostensibly, for our listeners. But the storyteller's reward doesn't come from them alone. Like Marcus, as we shape our story, our story shapes us; we gain new insights and meanings. Most important, we experience being alive. The experience is an encounter with one's own life and an appreciation of its unstoppable vigor.

As you begin your story performance, with a friend, say, over a quiet cup of coffee, you position your listener.

You paint in the background necessary for understanding, and then jump into the middle of your painting. But a teller is both subject and narrator. You are the story you tell. You are transforming the memory of an experience into a story through the act of telling it, like M. C. Escher's *Drawing Hands*, each creating the other. It is true to say that you draw the story; it is equally true to say that the story draws you—out of yourself, into new possibilities.

There are two listeners, your friend with the coffee and you. You are a listener to your own story. The story is in you, is you, yet some part of you listens as if for the first time to be sure your story impacts and makes sense. This strange dislocation from self grants perspective, one of the gifts of story and performance.

As you narrate and enact, your listener reacts emotionally to what she hears. She laughs, cries, and feels. Her emotions steer your story. The witness' unwavering attention, synchronized breathing, shared tears—exerts a powerful gravity. If your listener is open in unreserved acceptance and empathy to your story, she pulls you deeper into your tale. Your listener becomes co-Teller, and co-Subject, opening new vistas on the meanings in your story.

Events in your story can be so colored by the attention of your witness that your original experience is altered—after the fact. This contradicts our notion of the irreversibility of time and the factuality of incidents in the past, but such is the power of story. Sonia re-experienced NiNi, her younger self, as a hero. But NiNi—the memory of Sonia's young self—was changed, too. And in every subsequent re-telling of her story she, the subject, is no longer a victim, but emerges as the hero of her narrative. Something like this happened with Marcus, as well.

And this change in teller and subject came about through the synergy created through telling and witnessing. For three hours without break, Sonia and we held the space between us for her story to occupy. When it was done, something remarkable had transpired that relocated all of us. Together we had remade the story of a life.

Performance calls forth energy in a mystical world-changing way.

NiNi's liberation through story brings the energy of aliveness. As we exchanged roles—Teller, Subject, Witness—the energy of liberation and discovery increased with each shift. Humans long ago noticed the connection between feeling and action—emotion and motion. The feelings have to be engaged before anything changes in the external world. As we dance between the positions of a story—teller, subject, listener—the charge increases like a dynamo. Shifting positions within the magnetic field of story releases energy. We're here discussing the shifts between Witness, Subject, and Teller. But story has many such gaps that require such shifts. Each generates energy. With new knowledge we leap back to an earlier place in the story with enhanced understanding; we move forward in apprehension of what is about to happen; our hearts leap as we witness our effects on one another. We vault the gaps of story in the process of sense making—we jump to conclusions. Each leap charges the story performance field.

It's strange to think that an aesthetic act has the power to move a mountain, but it does. The emotional act of shifting between Teller, Witness, and Subject sets in motion human action. These shifts in perspective change the way we see the world and provide us with the energy to change the world we see. That is the power of story and performance. The full, unfettered act of sharing a story sets in motion shifts in perspective which liberate energy to change the world.

We remade Sonia's story. We transformed reality. Both statements mean the same thing. And both herald a tremendous release of energy, as in Einstein's equation. We might say $E=SP^2$, where E is the energy released, S is the shared story, and P, the people engaged as actors and witnesses in its performance. Multiplying and squaring terms illustrates the truth of Margaret Mead's assertion: the energy of a few people and a good story can change the world.

Performance of the Other

Aristotle knew it: "Man delights in Imitation." The little boy, despite his mother's annoyance, can't stop making faces in the chrome toaster at the breakfast table. Mimicry is only a few steps removed from something more genuine. When we play the storytelling game, first one person tells her story, "When I was a little girl..." then her partner tells it back in the first person. This is mimicry, too, but with a difference. Here the intention is to reflect deeply the other person, the part that touched us most. We are story beings, constantly thinking inside of and evolving our story and the stories of others.

The first power of performance is to show the self to the self. The second power is to show self and other to, well, self and other. To show the other, we must become the other. You stand inside your partner's story. You dress in her circumstance and feel the heft—where it presses down, where it lifts up—you become her. You speak her, "When I was a little girl..." The revelation of performance isn't becoming the other, it's remaining you and becoming the other *at the same time*. All of who you are remains sensible, as you pass through the other in performance. This is foundational to relationship, which we'll explore in the next chapter.

This fact is a crucial aspect of "the people's mic." Made famous by Occupy Wall Street and spread around the world, the people's mic is call and response. The audience amplifies the words of the speaker by repeating them. The people's mic came into use because authorities forbade electronic amplification, in an attempt to prevent disturbance and stifle communication. Instead, authorities gave rise to the circumstance that led not just to amplification, but to each person in the crowd, through performance, becoming the speaker. People don't merely repeat words, they repeat the gestural/emotional/vocal color of the speaker. They repeat the gestalt of the other, become the other. In the people's mic, willingness to listen and be deeply affected meets the human love of mimicry, with a transformational result. Simply put, playing the other changes us into the other by degrees; the psychological term is cognitive dissonance. To make a pond of followers into a river of leaders was not what was intended when the authorities banned amplification in Zuccotti Park. But such is the power of story performance on the performer herself.

All performance has this quality of gift and sacrifice. The performer is free to interpret the world, but that interpretation comes at the cost of alteration. In performance, the body is a riverbed shaped—torn away and built up—as performance moves through it. It is a candle burning at both ends, consumed as it illuminates. When we perform we are changed.

When Luis Valdez would go before Cesar Chavez into the communities and create performances, workers were eager to play the angry strikers. No one wanted to play the grape owners. No one wanted to play that hated and feared individual. The *campesino* who played the *patroncito* had to be talked into taking the role. After several performances in several communities, Valdez noticed something. The person who played the owner almost always became the indigenous leader of the local protest movement. Performing power— even the hated power of the oppressor—prepares the performer to lead.

The Story Jumps Into Us

We have explored in some detail how the teller steps out of herself and is met, inside the story, by the witness stepping out of herself. They merge in relationship, in the moment of its fertilization. This process of stepping out and merging is a fractal pattern that happens at all scales of magnification.

In a Community Performance, one person steps into another's story. Also, a group of people step into a story, and encounter each other in the same deep way. But it doesn't stop there. In a play made from the stories of a community, people encounter each other every which way, make connections and build relationships. Individual stories and performance experiences cement together to form a bridge. When this happens, and it *invariably* happens as folks respond authentically to the process, people experience themselves as a community. This happens in an afternoon Story Bridge workshop, or a year-long Community Performance project. Sharing stories, inhabiting stories, people experience community and each other as family.

But there is one more crucial dimension, which imparts its wisdom to the rest. Story itself steps out of itself and into other stories. Performance forms relationship between stories, which together reveal deep truths about the community. The result can be profound, can feel like the community itself, *as if it were a living thing,* used the performance to speak to its people.

> [T]hough we, as listeners have the illusion that we have jumped into the story, the story has actually jumped into us and uses our lives to tell out its story. (Prechtel, 2005)]

People from a small southern community, came together on a Friday night for *hors d'oeuvres,* drinks and conversation with Jules and Richard. In casual conversation, and in one brief circle conversation, this group of leaders (mayor, council person, heads of non-profits, churches, community organizations, educators) told us what challenged their community. "We live in silos." "The whites don't talk to the blacks." "The Catholics don't talk to the Protestants." "The coal operators and workers don't talk to the locals." This theme wasn't the only one, but it was a major motif. In the room that night were a group of people performing the silo theme. Most were white, middle class, and educated.

Next morning we sat in a large circle to hold a demonstration story circle. Two powerful stories we're performed—told and witnessed. The first was German immigrant tale, the second a Ukrainian Jew's story. Both performances counter-narrated the assertion made the night before that the community lived in silos. Once upon a time, at least, these two stories proclaimed a different sort of community from the one described the night before.

On Friday night, the community was saying "We're not inclusive, we don't know how to be inclusive." Then, on Saturday morning, as if by magic, up popped two stories—that fit naturally into a single performance—which showed that an appreciation of diversity is possible. Not just possible, but already performed, accomplished, by their forefathers and mothers.

What we witnessed happens with regularity. It doesn't happen when one or another individual or group attempts to manage or control the process. It's as if we placed our hands on a community Ouija board slide. If one person tries to push the planchette, the resulting story of stories is garbled and uninteresting—usually boring as well. But when all of us allow the planchette to move where it will, it points to a succession of stories that when *performed together* reveal a great deal about the community.

The rest of the Saturday we invited more stories through the Storytelling Game. That afternoon we asked the group to take the stories they'd chosen as their favorites and array them along a narrative arc, thereby creating a single performance. We didn't talk about the meaning of what was happening, not yet. We just asked them to put the stories in an order that "made sense," that "felt right."

To accomplish this, a person performed each story briefly. These eight or ten people stood in a line. These "Headliners," reminded us of which story each represented, like headlines, "The Drunk Driver," or "Her Father's Boots." People had seen and heard the performances, so these reminders were enough to bring the story to mind. Very quickly, prompted by Jules who asked simple questions like, "Which story feels like the climax?" the Headliners switched their order in line. In a few minutes, they stood in a specific order reflecting the group's consensus. Behind them on the board, we put these titles, as sticky notes, onto a narrative arc.

Next we asked, "Where would you want to put music? Dance? Ritual?" In another few minutes the arc filled up with full cast musical numbers, solo songs, dances, and full cast ritual elements. We were contributing an insight here and there, but mostly Jules and Richard were holding the space for the community to realize its own expression.

When everyone was satisfied, when it felt done, we rehearsed for an hour or so. Then we performed for anyone from the community who wanted to attend. There were shouts and hurrahs, belly laughs, and lots of tears. The performance ended with a naming of precious community members who were no longer alive, "Jakie Draper, I remember you."

After that, we invited audience and cast to sit in small groups and discuss the performance. Then we shared insights with the larger group. People were awed. Intentionally we'd created a performance from their stories, and then added songs as it felt right. Intentionally we'd made something that felt engaging, historically interesting, and above all entertaining. Our audience thought so, too.

Then we dove into what this performance was saying about us and our community *that we hadn't intended*. We examined the themes, metaphors and images that emerged from the performance. The play was filled with stories that counter-narrated the deficits which appeared on Friday night. To counter-narrate isn't to "answer." We could say that a story about friendship, "answered" a story about indifference. But "answers" kill the golden goose of story performance. A story isn't an answer, is it? It is much more. A story is a field of possibilities over which our minds and hearts can play.

We'd created all this, unintentionally. Some other intelligence, "serendipitous creativity," had intended this, not us.

The group of citizens and leaders recognized that their creation coded meanings that they'd never have known how to invoke if they'd set about to diagnose and fix their town. An intelligence asserted itself through the performance of the combined stories that was gentler, more engaging, and far wiser than any evaluation and prescription.

And it carried energy that made each person in the room want to continue and deepen the conversation about what was possible, and to widen the circle or relationship that would support possibility on its journey to positive change.

The late Harvard theologian, Gordon D. Kaufman, in his last book *In the Beginning...Creativity* distills a lifetime of thought about God. For him, the phrase most descriptive of those unaccountable moments of insight, awe, and wisdom is "serendipitous creativity." (Kaufman, 2004)

Conclusion

Performance begins with the powerful dislocation which tugs individuals out of ordinary consciousness toward a world seen before only in childhood play—a world in which "I" is one among others. Ego is challenged as the magnitudes of performance increase. A crisis point is reached beyond which the ego will not go. The crisis is unexpected and insurmountable. As the ego sees what is demanded, it rebels—cries, rages, retreats. At that moment, ego has found and is blocking the gate to personhood. Without ego, the self would never have found this passage. Ego was the guide to this point, but ego can go no farther. The moment self agrees to surrender and go forward, straight into the jaws of that which it feared, ego drops off. Self feels the dead weight slide off as it exits the little garden of its previous life and moves into the world of others, where "I" becomes "we," in full personhood.

Personhood enables us *fully* to perform the other, in full access to our creativity. The performance of the other is perhaps the richest way humans can *know*. We can visit a museum and stand before a painted king, release our ego, and occupy his body, its tension and posture, fit his face to ours, look out through his eyes...and know something of his world. We can release ego and be again a baby at its birth, or a granite cliff, or love itself. Performance is a sense beyond our five senses, a way of knowing which can lead to compassion and relationship with everything we perform.

Why on the Story Bridge does performance come before relationship? Early on, we thought what we were seeing was folks coming together around stories and then building relationships that enabled them to perform together. Story, relationship, performance, in that order. As we looked more carefully, we realized that people sharing stories never became people in relationship until they went through the ego-slaying experience of performance. Story had to be performed before relationship could appear. That clued us to the true place and power of performance. Powerful performance may not only mean standing on a dark stage in a bright light before a thousand enthralled admirers. It may mean something more subtle. As we step into the time-binding world of story, we step into performance and out of ourselves. I step into an encounter with you. That merging *is* relationship. Story and performance are the parents of relationship and change. Through story you perform difference. You find courage and possibility—like Marcus and the *campesinos*—to become something new in the world.

When we engage with each other's stories in performance, the result is a relationship that transcends mere understanding. Words like "empathy" or "compassion" better express the connection. Once sensed, it sets up a longing in us to actualize it as our ground of being together.

> *"Our goal is to create a beloved community," said Dr. King, "and this will require a qualitative change in our souls as well as a quantitative change in our lives."*

For twenty years, through the sharing of stories in performance, we've witnessed ordinary folks catch the spark of beloved community and want to bend their places and themselves toward its beckoning ideal.

THE SECOND PIER OF THE STORY BRIDGE SUPPORTS
RELATIONSHIPS AND BONDS TEAMS. WHEN HUMANS TELL
AND WITNESS STORIES, WE CONNECT QUICKLY AND DEEPLY.
THIS IS A PROFOUND TRUTH, ROOTED IN THE REALITY THAT
ONLY WHEN WE WITNESS WHAT SOMEONE HAS LIVED
THROUGH—MEET THEIR PERSONHOOD WITH OUR
PERSONHOOD—DO WE FULLY APPRECIATE THEM. WHEN WE
EMBODY OUR STORIES TOGETHER, WE BECOME A
COMMUNITY. THE EXPERIENCE IS FRIENDSHIP, LOVE, AND
FAMILY.

CHAPTER THREE: RELATIONSHIP

In the center of performance is a mystery. Why it should be, we don't know. But humans are constituted in such a way that when the performer is freed from the egoistic need to be "the star," something altogether different is liberated.

Once slain, the ego is reborn as Hermes, the soul guide. When self, stripped of ego, undertakes the journey, ego (Hermes) accompanies. In its role as Hermes, it guides the performer on the journey, and remembers the way home.

For fifteen years our choreographer has been Kevin Iega Jeff, who, at 6'7", is a perfect physical form, a god among mortals. His very first job was dancing a lead on Broadway when he was barely old enough to drive. Today, there is no finer choreographer in the nation. Surely, reason enough for ego. But Iega's ego is in the role of Hermes. Iega will let go of his most brilliant idea without a second thought if it serves the collaborative. But Iega knows his boundaries; he knows which patterns serve the growing collective creation; he knows he must devote much of his day to self-care if he is to be fully present in the hours of creation in the rehearsal room. All these boundary issues are looked after by ego-as-Hermes.

If ego is not the hero, who is? Dr. King said it, Soul. Soul grows through performance. Remember the story of Arthur and Merlin? Merlin, the guide, showed the boy Arthur how truly to understand the world—through *becoming* its creatures. Deep mimicry is knowing *as the other knows*. Informed by intuition, mimicry helps the soul shape-shift. High performance is shape-shifting, profound and transformational. Through his journeys, Wart becomes king.

Self travels through performance to meet its higher self and other souls in relationship.

This is the reason that the stories performed in the story-to-change process are stories that come from the people themselves. They are not enacting or trying to embody an archetype or hero. They are not creating characters foreign to their experience but, rather, re-creating characters they know, if not personally, then at least within their culture. How do I act like a moonshiner? Ask Jerry; his grandfather ran liquor. How do I act like a sheriff in this story? Ask cast member, Buddy, who is a state trooper. How do I stand in the shoes of the women who marched for Civil Rights in Lavonia, Georgia? Ask Barbara; she was twenty years old when she took part in that march. How do I become the Confederate woman who baked bread for the Union troops? Ask 95 year old Sydney; his grandmother remembered her mother doing this and told Sydney about it. The people we seek to know and understand better are with us, in the cast, or in the community.

As we stand in their shoes, in performance, we get to know, at a bone depth, who they are, what their values are, and what they believe. A transformed understanding of one another emerges. And it emerges not through books, not through debates, not through history classes, but through the embodiment that performance fundamentally is. This understanding bypasses our thoughts, our presuppositions, and our prejudices. It is more direct, it is *feeling*. Once we have embodied and empathized with another's story, their story lives within us. We know something we didn't before. What was not possible before begins to be possible now. A community fills with understanding and empathy for all its people, and grows capable of doing great things for itself.

This community sees through multiple eyes, and feels through many hands and hearts the desires, needs, and dreams of everyone. With this collective local knowledge, the people can create positive change.

This does not mean that people on opposing sides will drop their differences. It does mean that there is relationship between these people, a ground of appreciation and understanding, a place to build.

Taking Sides, or Taking a Closer Look

Mark and James seemed destined for disagreement. James is the executive director of a progressive non-profit and Mark is the city manager. James acknowledges the town's significant financial and material support for the project. Though sometimes the city's take-charge attitude overwhelms the emerging organic community process James supports. When volunteer leadership is lacking, Mark moves forward anyway, and that feels controlling to James.

Mark experiences James as a type. He recognizes James' type because he's been a city manager for more than twenty years. James is the difficult-to-please, highly vocal citizen. James has complimented Mark on his vision and perception, but he is equally quick to point out what he thinks isn't working. The city is filled with things that made James want to move here five years ago, and Mark is directly or indirectly responsible for many of those things. Mark is open to criticism because he isn't reactive; he is proactive. He sees possibilities for his community and goes after them. So does James. They're deeply alike in their goals, though not in their methods.

Mark and James both joined the project for its inaugural performance. Not yet knowing them, we innocently cast them to play the same role, a through-character, who appears in several scenes. They shared responsibility to make sure that one or the other of them was at every rehearsal and performance. If one missed a rehearsal, the other filled in. They watched each other grow in the role. Both were devoted cast members, community elders, exemplifying how, through sharing a role, to make Community Performance work with their busy lives. No two men are more deeply devoted to their community and to the project. Both are beloved.

We would like to say that Mark and James have become good friends, that standing in each other's shoes has given them empathy for each other, and that empathy has led to a deep friendship. We'd like to say that, but it wouldn't quite be true. The empathy has changed them both. Sharing the role, each has stood in the other's shoes, and come to appreciate the different ways of working for a better community. By being each other's second, they have taken a second look, given a second chance. Their second sight enables them to see the challenge and the ally each is to the other. Their eyes are fixed on the same place, the beloved community toward which each works.

Mark and James, through the new relationship that emerged between them, were able to find a new way to experience each other. This happens not just to a couple of people during the process, but to most. With these new relationships and connections, a space of safety and creativity is born. Once in relationship, we no longer seek to prove our side, but rather share hopes and desires and needs. Relationship helps drive out the "stopping energy" of the reflexive "no" that becomes habit to those who spend time fighting for a cause. Relationship allows us to listen to the other. Even if we don't agree with them, our relationship, and the respect that goes with it, stops us from discounting the other or shouting him down. When this happens, solutions, that were not able to be seen before, become visible. Possibilities open up.

A Circle Of Hands: Relationship Allows Painful Stories To Be Understood More Fully

Valada told her story in Sanford, Florida, about the first experience of the pain of racism. African American, Valada grew up next door to a white family. She and the little neighbor girl would play together. Valada's family went on vacation and while they were gone, a fence went up. When Valada arrived home, she went out back to play with her friend. They could see each other, but they were separated. She called, but her friend didn't come. Valada called again, and finally the white girl called back

"No."

Valada said, "Why?"

And the little girl replied, "Because. You're black."

Fifty years later, the story was difficult for Valada to perform. It was also difficult for the mothers and grandmothers of the girls who played Little Valada and her neighbor. But the girls had no trouble. They were playing *at* the roles, not inhabiting them. One of the mothers spoke. She did not want the scene to be something cute played by the sweet girls. She asked to stop rehearsal. She had us form a tight circle and extend our arms.

"See our hands? See all of these colors? God made them all. Which color do you think is God's favorite?"

A girl said, "That's a weird question."

"Yes, it is," she continued, "but when I was a little girl, and when Miss Valada was little, we were not allowed to do a lot of things because our skin color was dark. We had to sit in the balcony upstairs. We couldn't go in a lot of restaurants. We couldn't even use the same bathroom or drink out of the same water fountain."

The children in the room—black, brown, white, pink, tan, and mocha latte—stood rapt in the story. Some hearing of discrimination for the first time. Moms and grandmothers began to add to the story. They wanted these kids really to know and understand how important it was that they were not only telling this story, but feeling it, too. There were questions and answers. And while lines were not being read, *this was rehearsal.* Inside of the word rehearsal is the word "rehear." The story was being re-heard and re-told until everyone in the room *knew.* When the lines on the stage resumed, everyone was different, those on the stage and those watching. What allowed the understanding? The relationship that had formed in the performance process. This wasn't a debate about race. It was the telling of personal experiences and stories, of people we could talk with, touch, and care for. And in so doing, we applied a balm to very old wounds. When this story was finally performed on stage, its tellers, and those who identified with them, felt heard and honored.

Not In My Backyard

In Uptown Chicago, Bill owned a gorgeous, upscale condo in a mixed-income neighborhood. It was the early 90's and the beginning of the gentrification of the area. During this time, Uptown was notorious for being the last stop on the line for those leaving jails and mental hospitals, so there were many people on the streets, and many single room occupancy buildings (SROs) to house the formerly homeless. Groups formed to push this element out of the neighborhood, often called "NIMBY" organizations (Not In My Back Yard). Bill headed one of these. He wanted to protect the investment he worked hard for, he wanted to transform the "social service ghetto" that he and others saw Uptown becoming.

The Community Performance project Scrap Mettle SOUL formed during this period. SMS's mission was to present stories of urban life (SOUL) from the entire community, including the homeless. There was so much diversity: the homeless, those supporting the homeless, those opposed, those who supported the police, those who were out to expose police corruption, little ethnic enclaves speaking over one hundred languages, and families of every kind trying to make a living and raise their kids. A gateway community, Uptown, 60640, has been called the most diverse zip code in the United States. In the middle of this stood Scrap Mettle SOUL, literally in the middle, because SMS did not take sides. In it, you would find Bill, passionately telling the story of his days building IBM as an executive, and building a life for himself and his wife in this neighborhood he loved so much; you would also meet Geraldine, a former bag lady, who found Uptown to be the neighborhood where she felt most comfortable. You'd also meet Barbara, an amazing organizer, who's economic situation led her to live in subsidized housing; Stephan, a brilliant PhD, bi-polar, formerly homeless; and Joe who lived in the SRO that Bill was trying to close.

Bill and Joe were cast to sing a duet. Center state, the NIMBY Bill singing with the SRO chap he didn't want in his backyard; in turn, politically active Joe, dancing with "the man."

As the two rehearsed a relationship formed. Instead of saying "you're wrong" for thinking this way, each one, in the context of safety and trust that the work provided, was able to appreciate the other. Stories emerged. Questions arouse, and a sincere desire to learn about the other. "Bill, why don't you want me in the neighborhood?" With the first question, people, not postures, started to speak.

Bill did not leave his NIMBY organization. And Joe did not stop his political action. But things changed at a personal level. Joe was able to see Bill other than as the enemy. They would even meet and have lunch. Bill saw Joe, Stephan, and Barbara, not as subsidized housing residents, but as people. He recognized Barbara's skills and referred her to a better paying job, and this allowed her to keep the home she was about to lose.

The individual connections allowed change to happen—person by person. It was not a revolution, but it was life changing for those individuals, as they moved from "I" to "We."

Relationship Moves Us From "I" to "We"

Beloved community enables relationships which could not exist without its contradictory centrifugal and centripetal forces. The diverse community of the Jonesborough Yarn Exchange is able to hold Mark and James in relationship and release their magnificent and very different synergistic energies. The Sanford play tells the story of pain; in order to be released from it, the actors had to travel more deeply into it, to come through it. Bill, Joe, Barbara, and Stephan became different people to each other. That is the journey, across the bridge, in relationship.

We travel the Story Bridge as "We," not "I." Impossible juxtapositions, challenging relationships, character transformations become possible. One doesn't take the journey for oneself, but with and for others. More is possible. One crosses the bridge for generations to come, for all of us, because we are one. And in that "one," oneself is safely transported.

In Middletown, Connecticut, we encountered the deepest, most concise meaning of the journey. David Blumenkrantz, our friend, colleague, and the father of the modern rites of passage movement, says:

> *"We've gotten all tangled up in careers, houses, and commercialism, and forgotten the core purpose of community. Our job is to raise the children."*

That's why we must move from "I" to "We." We can only do that together. It takes the whole village.

THE THIRD PIER IS CONVERSATION. ENERGIZED, BY MOVING INTO EACH OTHERS' STORIES AND INTO EACH OTHER'S HEARTS, WE WANT TO TALK. WE MOVE EASILY INTO CONVERSATION AROUND IMPORTANT QUESTIONS. CRITICAL CONVERSATION ALSO OFTEN BEGINS WITH STORY. WE LAY OUR HEART STORIES SIDE BY SIDE, FURTHER DEEPEN OUR CONNECTIONS, THEN DISCUSS WHAT IS POSSIBLE IN OUR SHARED FUTURE THAT WASN'T POSSIBLE BEFORE. FROM THESE CONVERSATIONS WE CAN HARVEST COLLECTIVE WISDOM.

CHAPTER FOUR: CONVERSATION

A Really Good Conversation

For six years we've done one-day workshops with the participants in the Building Creative Communities Conference held each February in Colquitt, GA, and co-sponsored by the Swamp Gravy Institute and Florida State University.

Each year a new group of FSU faculty, graduate students from urban planning, art therapy, social work, and a few other fields, join community folks from around the United States to explore with Joy Jinks, Karen Kimbrel, Richard, and other founders of Swamp Gravy. Our purpose is to utilize our experience in community creativity to help members of other communities and students more fully to engage creative possibilities for community action.

Every year we lead groups of about sixty in a one-day creation process. We start with the stories they carry with them, the stories of their lived experience. We ask them to remember, for instance, a time "when your life changed." Starting with sixty stories, the participants winnow quickly to ten or so. Working together we order these stories into the shape of performance (ascending, complicating action leading to climax and falling action—the narrative arc described in Chapter Two). Then we added music, costumes, props, and lights and perform for a local audience that night on the Swamp Gravy stages. It's an exhausting, engaging, revelatory process. It causes us to care deeply about one another, bond as a group, and it reveals what collectively was on our minds and hearts.

The process is:

STORY → *PERFORMANCE* → *RELATIONSHIP*

Contrast that with the Story Bridge process:

STORY → *PERFORMANCE* → *RELATIONSHIP* → *CONVERSATION* → *COMMITTED ACTION*

At the Staging Change Institute, held recently in Jonesborough, TN we did the same performance process, then connected it to the World Café model of conversation. We carried the energy and insight of the story/performance/relationship process, into catalytic conversations around important topics. Conversation led to individual and group action plans.

The difference confirmed the intuition we'd shared from the moment we'd met Juanita Brown and David Isaacs, the co-founders of the World Café. Juanita and David discovered in our process energy and insight which can activate dynamic conversations. We discovered, in theirs, a way of channeling the caring, energy, and commitment of story performance into community change. Both of us realized that our processes engaged story in powerful ways. The Community Performance part and the World Café part were both animated by story sharing among the participants. The Staging Change Institute, by no coincidence, took place at the International Storytelling Center, in Jonesborough, Tennessee.

For years, before this discovery, we'd created unique and powerful plays for our audiences, and moving and inspiring processes for participants. At the conclusion of a season, the energy of the cast fairly exploded. Cast members didn't want to stop but they had no place to go, and nothing to do. It felt as if something might burst, almost dangerous in its intensity, like a tsunami hitting the back wall of the theater; pent-up energy with no place to go. We'd spent the year listening to, embodying, performing, filling up with all the inspiring stories of the community's past that pointed at what might be possible in its future. At the end of each season, we wanted to do more, but didn't know how.

Over the years, in different communities, we saw ancillary activities spawned—youth companies, after school programs, Christmas and summer shows, community gardens, entirely new theater organizations. Some of them thrived, but time showed us that this wasn't the direction our energy wanted to move. We weren't being asked to create another kind of theater. We were being asked to leap a chasm from Community Performance to community participation. We were being asked to create another kind of community. None of us knew how.

Then we met Juanita and David. The first thing they wanted to know was "What is the experience?" They came to half a dozen rehearsals and as many performances of the Jonesborough Yarn Exchange. They steeped themselves in our process because they were curious. We became a learning community.

World Café is a simple and powerful conversational *process* which promotes and supports constructive dialogue, accesses collective intelligence, and surfaces innovative possibilities for action, particularly in groups that are larger than most traditional dialogue approaches are designed to accommodate. (Brown & Isaacs, The World Cafe: Shaping Our Futures Through Conversations That Matter, 2005, p. 3) The process has spread literally around the world where in communities and organizations large and small it cross-pollinates ideas, fosters engagement, and builds sustainable futures.

After learning the basics of conversational leadership, the cast of the Jonesborough Yarn Exchange hosted a World Café dialogue on our lived experience, as a company. We hosted another World Café following a community performance toward the end of the run and invited the audience to join in. Our season ended but instead of stopping dead, our energy bridged from the theater to the Staging Change Institute. There, JYE cast members spent an exciting investigatory weekend working with professionals and community experts in the community-based arts and dialogue fields. After story circles and performances, after we'd become friends, we took our experiences into conversations about how to make a positive difference in our own communities.

In twenty years of doing community performances, and workshops too numerable to count, we'd learned to anticipate the outcome: people loved the process and wanted to do more plays, but if circumstance didn't allow that, the energy gradually dissipated and we went our separate ways. The energy pushed folks to create a new Community Performance project, or it petered out. But with the Jonesborough Yarn Exchange cast, as we moved into conversation, we had a different experience.

At the Institute, one of the story prompts we used is called "Beautiful River."

*The Beautiful River arose in the Beautiful
Mountains and flowed to the Beautiful Sea. When
the Beautiful River came to the Terrible Desert it
looked around in despair, "How will I get across?"
The Beautiful Clouds heard this cry and came to the
rescue. "Don't worry, Beautiful River," they said,
"We'll take you up and carry you to the Beautiful
Sea." "But what will become of me, my remarkable
length, my sparkling depths?" "Why you'll
evaporate, of course," the Clouds said. Beautiful
River didn't like this at all, Beautiful River was
terrified. The Beautiful Clouds said, "You have two
choices, Beautiful River. You can pour yourself
into the Terrible Desert and disappear forever, or we
will lift you up and carry you transformed to the
Beautiful Sea."*

This story prompt helps the listener move intuitively
to the story she will tell. All of us have lived the archetypal
passages of the Beautiful River story. We've danced along
our way, been threatened by obstacles, and accepted or
refused the call to transformation.

One choice for the Beautiful River is to pour its
energy uselessly into the Terrible Desert. For years we'd used
this story prompt, but didn't recognize ourselves in it.
Working with communities we had developed a process for
gathering the droplets of story into rivulets, and those into
creeks, and the creeks of story into a Beautiful River of
community story, performance, and relationship. For years
we poured that creative energy into the Terrible Desert
because we didn't know what else to do with it.

We had been pursuing a means to take the energy of
creativity out of the theater, into the community, David and

Juanita were pursuing their intuitions about the power of story. We met half way along the bridge we didn't know we were building. We thrilled with the energy of our first meeting. It took us a few weeks to realize intellectually what we'd felt instantly. Communities could carry story, performance, and relationship all the way to committed change, through the transforming power of conversation.

After the Staging Change Institute, after working our shared processes for a weekend, Juanita and David had a realization. Our processes were not only complementary, but together they had the capacity to mobilize community members in ways neither of us had anticipated in our earlier work. Community Performance and World Café

> *depend on a safe and welcoming space, and a prompt to encourage deep sharing from personal experience. Storytelling empowers both processes. People come to care for one another as they perform together (telling and listening are performing). The group winnows their experience in successive rounds. At the end, in plenary/performance, the wisdom is harvested.*

The Story Bridge is two spans joined together, both including story as a key component. It is illuminating to us to hear from Juanita and David that the conversation part of the bridge is enriched through story. When people engage one another authentically, the likelihood of a powerful conversation is enhanced. As David reminds us, the deepest conversations are about meeting, encountering the other person, in a place beyond words. We think of Rumi:

*Beyond our ideas of right-doing and wrong-doing,
there is a field. I'll meet you there.*

*When the soul lies down in that grass, the world is
too full to talk about.*

*Ideas, language, even the phrase 'each other'
doesn't make sense any more.*

> *Jelaluddin Rumi*

We realize that the place in which community (successful teams, loving congregations, creative ensembles, etc.) is made possible isn't a *reason-able* place, but a place beyond words. There we realize our care for one another, our interdependence, our reciprocal creation of each other. "*Ubuntu,*" as David says, "I am because we are." That's what we experience in both processes.

David reflects on some of the elements which support effective World Café conversations:

At a Café session we pay a great deal of attention to:

- *Setting up the room to actually look like a café.*
- *Having the intimacy of small café table conversations within a larger space where each table could feel connected to the larger whole.*
- *Using art, music, and greenery.*
- *Using volunteers as greeters and hosts.*
- *Using the language of "hosts," "travelers" and "guests" during the Café rounds to encourage a spirit of mutual hospitality and friendship.*

- *Encouraging more living systems images through the use of language like "planting seeds" and "cross-pollinating of ideas."*
- *Going out into the audience to be with the participants during the conversation of the whole.*
- *Wearing informal yet appropriate attire.*
- *Using hand drawn graphics rather than Power Point presentations.*
- *Giving gifts to each participant.*

These may seem like simple things but they are rarely done in the context of supporting collective intelligence and knowledge evolution in organizations. We feel that it is critical to shift the context within which people explore the core questions in organizations and communities. There is something, for example, about the core image of a café that evokes, even across cultures, a common set of conversational responses — ones that are more creative, playful, curious, honest, intimate, and real than the responses evoked in most formal business meetings and hotel-based off-site retreats. Creating a warm, inviting, and informal space like a café is one way of shifting the context to encourage more generative conversations to emerge. When this context, (a Café setting or other informal environment) is accompanied by a clear and creative process (the Café method or other self-organizing methodology) that includes cross-pollination and linking of diverse ideas around a content (strategic questions) that really matter to people, then you've got the possibility for coherence of thought to become visible at a collective level.

*[Interview with Juanita Brown and David Isaacs,
June 23, 2012]*

Before meeting Juanita and David and learning about
the power of World Café conversations, we'd taken intuitive
first steps with community performance casts. We couldn't
help talking about the things that happened between us, as a
result of the process. But now we were able to go farther.
We had a conceptual framework to help us take our next
steps. Using simple tools—simple in concept—the
Jonesborough Yarn Exchange held its first World Café. We
began with the question.

What is happening here?

When conducting a Café, it's useful to state and re-
state the question in slightly different forms as folks are
absorbing it. "What has been your experience in this process?
How has the project connected with you, meaningfully?
What stands out?" The magic of the Café process is to stay
inside questions, not answers, to hone those questions, to ask
them from different angles, vantages, and points of view.

What are we forgetting?

Who isn't in the room? What would they ask?

*Looking back five years from now, what would we
know to ask?*

Can you hear the performance quality in these
questions? Like story, they ask you to dislocate from your

rooted presence in self, time, and place, and to step into difference, to experience the world from a new vantage. Fresh thinking is diverse thinking. When the people in the room are diverse—generations, abilities, cultures—questions are interpreted from many points of view, generating rich responses. Toke Møller, co-founder of the Art of Hosting, which has introduced the World Café and other conversational methodologies to leaders across the globe, says,

> *Effective action often comes out if you are exploring a question that is really alive for people. The paradoxical thing is that action almost always comes out of a conversation that has life in it, but it doesn't have to be the primary stated goal."* (Brown *& Isaacs, The World Cafe: Shaping Our Futures Through Conversations That Matter, 2005, p. 81)*

At the first World Café with the Jonesborough Yarn Exchange, we used the following elements of the World Café process: for twenty minutes, at tables of four, people shared their initial responses to the question "What is happening here?." Then they thanked one another, one person remained at the table to host three new arrivals, and the other three sat down at three different tables. For an additional fifteen or twenty minutes, these groups of four built off what they'd found important in the previous conversation. Then they switched, and did the same thing one more time. At the conclusion of the third round, the Café hosts (one a 63 year old man, the other a 17 year old woman) asked the whole group:

What's alive for you from these conversations?

Below we've grouped the responses from this Café:

- Yesterday I took time with someone (a stranger) I'd normally have passed by. We bonded through her story.
- I'm choosing to listen to the stories of others.
- Everyone has a story, and everyone is listening now.
- I knew everyone has a story, but before I didn't necessarily respect or value it as it deserved.
- Our experience typically stays within micro-communities. Here it ripples out.
- There is the quivering potential. Oh, gosh, what's next?
- We're on the brink of a special thing, different from theater.
- The goal is good performance, but the goal is not the performance. Performance is a tool to unite us.
- It's our personal stories, and those of a community that we all love that's made this experience what it is.
- There's something here, I can't put my finger on it. Yes, it is, it's love.
- When PC was going to do that role the other night and Cassandra and Toby pitched in to help him feel better, that's love.
- Just treating someone as if they matter.
- Something that comes to my mind is investment.
- Setting aside politics, religion, cultural background, this can overcome that.
- This place matters.
- Blessing upon blessing.

- As a transitional pastor I was trained to ask people what they think of an issue. If only I knew then what I know now. Now I'd ask, "Tell me how your story is affected by this." Thinking leads us to "right" or "wrong." Story is your truth. No one can take it away from you. What has happened in the last few months right here is truths.
- A place to celebrate our differences.
- Around retiring age we start to ignore people. In other cultures they are the wisdom leaders. Here we give new life to their stories.

Through their experience of local stories and shared performance, relationships had grown. Points of difference became points of light illuminating new possibilities. "I" had become "we." As "we" took stock of that shift, all realized that more was possible than had previously been conceived. People began to sense a way of being in community at a far higher level of support, sustainability, creativity, and joy.

A challenge for all conversation technologies is not immediately to problem-solve. People, new to the dialogue technologies, want to jump to conclusions. It feels as if we should be able to harvest the wisdom and move to action, right away. We are discovering that conversations embody different qualities. For example, in divergent conversations, we notice more, bring out more observations, share ever more deeply. We listen, observe, and appreciate, in *divergent* conversations. There are also conversations that spot emerging patterns, discover "Ah-ha!" moments, notice trends, draw conclusions, and formulate action plans. These are *convergent* conversations.

Juanita is gifted at discovering patterns across a field of observations. She can classify the comments coming from a group into categories, and spot what is beginning to appear. There are Juanitas in every group and they need to be encouraged to use their skills. But all of us have this ability. We find that convergence happens as we begin to focus the range of ideas that are generated in the divergent mode. David is gifted at divergent conversation. He encourages our minds to stay open to possibilities, listen deeply, learn the language of others, and to appreciate the unique contributions of each member.

Divergence is the perfect prologue to convergence. As a host, your ability to encourage people to develop their divergent muscles can result in more convergent outcomes, and provide the opportunity for developing solutions. People often want to move from reflecting on their discoveries, like the list above, to answering the unspoken question: "What do we do now?" Answering this question validates the time and effort the group has spent. Your job as a conversational host is to help them focus on the opportunities that are made visible through their discoveries. People who care about one another, who have shared deeply in each other's stories, and plumbed together deep questions about their shared experience, are *already* taking committed action for their community. Their shift in attitude is transformational; seeing more in each other and the community around us *is* community change, isn't it.

The divergent conversation process feels like the gradual build-up of electrical charge in a cloud. The cloud doesn't have to worry about making lightning. That will happen by itself. Convergent thinking often strikes lightning out of a broad field of divergent observations.

Suddenly, toward the end of our large-group conversation, a core idea crystallized as if from nowhere....Although it was one person who spoke it out, she voiced our collective understanding of the deep...purpose that had brought us together in the first place.

The idea was simple, but for us, profound. Maybe that's how insight is....Suddenly we all saw our mutual commitment....The unexpected collective "surprise" that emerged that day....was a turning point in our strategic direction for the future. (Brown & Isaacs, The World Cafe: Shaping Our Futures Through Conversations That Matter, 2005, p. 116)

Before the Ah-ha moments, as people share themselves in conversation, the most important thing is already happening. "Buberian meeting," David calls it, after Martin Buber's exhortation to meet the other as a sacred being, a "Thou," not an "It." This is the sentiment of Rumi, meeting in a field beyond categories of separation. Joseph Campbell asserts that it isn't meaning that we're in search of, but the experience of being alive. Meaning is convergence. The experience of being alive is being at play, living in fullness, gratitude, experiencing the supporting net of relationships, or being a child and finding 52 uses for a paperclip. Divergence.

On the near side of the Story Bridge, the Storytelling Game enables a group of four people to choose a story to share through performance. On the far side of the bridge, in conversation, a group of four will again share stories. This time the group is listening for essence and the emerging group story that will lead to the other sort of performance:

committed action. The first round of story led to performance on the stage, the second round of story leads to performance in the streets, on the playground, or in the boardroom. Through the double process of story that is the Bridge, we use story first to energize us with what might be, and then to actualize what is possible.

Why go through this two-step process with story? Why not move immediately to action? For the same reason that astronauts, athletes, and armies practice. Practice, in the disciplines of story, performance and relationship, takes place in an as-if world where consequences are less but in which relationships grow strong. Actions can be rehearsed and perfected. The practice period also raises the energy of the whole system in preparation for action.

Before entering the practice field of story-performance-relationship, there may be insufficient energy in the system to accomplish group change. The only time when this isn't true is in times of crisis when an army invades, a hurricane hits, or a fire sweeps the town. Unfortunately, in such times we are in a reactive instead of proactive mode. We are problem-oriented instead of solution-oriented. Utilizing the story-to-change process, people gather around their stories. The wisdom in the story performance energizes and bonds us, then moves us through conversation to a creative, solution-focused approach leading to committed action.

Questions for All Seasons*

Here is a series of generative questions that we and other colleagues have found useful to stimulate new knowledge and creative thinking in a wide variety of situations around the world. Look at these questions to stimulate your own thinking about questions related to your own specific situation. Play. Use your imagination.

Questions for Focusing Collective Attention on Your Situation

- What question, if answered, could make the most difference to the future of (your specific situation)?
- What's important to you about (your specific situation) and why do you care?
- What draws you/us to this inquiry?
- What's our intention here? What's the deeper purpose (the big "why") that is really worthy of our best effort?
- What opportunities can you see in (your specific situation)?
- What do we know so far/still need to learn about (your specific situation)?
- What are the dilemmas/opportunities in (your specific situation)?
- What assumptions do we need to test or challenge here in thinking about (your specific situation)?
- What would someone who had a very different set of beliefs than we do say about (your specific situation)?

Questions for Connecting Ideas and Finding Deeper Insight

- What's taking shape? What are you hearing underneath the variety of opinions being expressed? What's in the center of the table?
- What's emerging here for you? What new connections are you making?
- What has real meaning for you from what you've heard? What surprised you? What challenged you?

- What's missing in this picture so far? What is it we're not seeing? What do we need more clarity about?
- What's been your/our major learning, insight, or discovery so far?
- What's the next level of thinking we need to do?
- If there was one thing that hasn't yet been said in order to reach a deeper level of understanding/clarity, what would that be?

Questions that Create Forward Momentum

- What would it take to create change on this issue?
- What could happen that would enable you/us to feel fully engaged and energized about (your specific situation)?
- What's possible here and who cares? (rather than "What's wrong here and who's responsible?)
- What needs our immediate attention going forward?
- If our success was completely guaranteed, what bold steps might we choose?
- How can we support each other in taking the next steps? What unique contribution can we each make?
- What challenges might come our way and how might we meet them?
- What conversation, if begun today, could ripple out in a way that created new possibilities for the future of (your situation)?
- What seed might we plant together today that could make the most difference to the future of (your situation)?

*Reprinted, with permission, from *The Art of Powerful Questions*. (Vogt, Brown, & Isaacs, 2003)

THE RISING ENERGY OF STORY, PERFORMANCE, RELATIONSHIP, AND CONVERSATION MOVES TO SOLUTIONS; THE ANCHORAGE THAT COMPLETES THE STORY BRIDGE IS COMMITTED ACTION. ACTION TAKES PEOPLE OUT INTO THEIR COMMUNITIES, DRIVEN THERE BY PASSION FOR THE TASK, AND THEIR DEEP FEELING FOR THEIR PLACE AND EACH OTHER. STORY, PERFORMANCE AND RELATIONSHIP REVEAL AND DEFINE THE INTENTIONAL, LIVING ORGANISM: THE SHARED COMMUNITY IN MOTION. CONVERSATION DISCOVERS ITS PURPOSE. COMMITTED ACTION MAKES IT HAPPEN. ACTION FINISHES ONE STORY AND BEGINS THE NEXT. ACTION CHANGES THE STORY AND CHANGES THE FUTURE.

CHAPTER FIVE: COMMITTED ACTION

Dracula -- The Accidental First Crossing

Dracula was the first time Richard crossed the Story Bridge, but we would not recognize that fact for 30 years. He knew something had happened. But for many years he couldn't explain it, couldn't see it fully. The community of Steamboat Springs, Colorado, where the original play was produced, crossed the Bridge to a changed place. But an explanation of how that happened awaited developments in story, performance, and conversation. When it happened, Richard wasn't sure what he was experiencing. He just knew he wanted to make it happen again.

Steamboat Repertory Theatre was in residence at the old train depot in Steamboat Springs; actors and audiences got used to 100-car coal trains shaking the building and interrupting performances. But as we began rehearsals for the 1980-81 season, we got word from the building inspector that the depot had been shaken too much and could no longer be used as a theater. Richard was a young artistic director with a season of four plays, a company of actors, designers, and technicians, and no theater. He quickly went to the high school and scheduled two of the productions into their theater, and the third at a local hotel. But that was it. No more space. Dracula was homeless.

Driving the streets of Ski Town USA didn't take long, Steamboat Springs had only five thousand full time residents. Very quickly he realized that the only big buildings were churches. Richard parked in front of the A-frame Methodist Church and went in to see Rev. Harold Raines.

He told Harold the story of Dracula as he intended to present it, as an allegory of faith and community. Dracula isn't about the flashy monster who sucks blood, he said, but the clutch of humans who have to overcome their differences to defeat the monster. Richard saw Dracula as a play about people learning to be in community despite themselves. Their double task was to find camaraderie, and finish-off the Count. Bickering suitors, an aging sexist professor, a callow and silly girl, and an impatient modern woman were pitted against a deathless demon of near-infinite power. The stage setting, an overhanging webbing of Gothic arches like bat's wings, shadowed everything in Dracula's pall. Around the edges, always present, would be Dracula's minions painted and draped to resemble stone statuary. They changed the setting, hovered spookily, and made it very clear that the humans had no chance. But directly above the central altar of the chapel, set in bas relief, was Archangel Michael with sword in hand. Michael, casting bat-winged Lucifer out of heaven, symbolized the play's hope.

Richard told Harold the story about faith and community, and he immediately understood how it could serve his congregation; this twelve-stepping, ex-alcoholic, man of spirit knew about battling demons. His congregation, he told me, had fallen upon easy times. A light had gone out and Harold wanted it back.

Together we plotted a revival. We transformed the sanctuary very, very carefully. Installing the set was an act of reverence. Every nail we didn't put into that place drove home the fact that we were working with sacred space. It made us act with reverence. It made us honor, it made us take care, in the same way we need to revere the story, and honor it. The First Methodist Church of Steamboat Springs was either an old A-frame where a bunch of people crouched piously once a week, or was a place where the folk conversed with mystery. The choice was ours, every one of ours, to make in every moment. Were we at work in a space where nothing mattered, or where every action had consequence? The scruffy bunch of long-haired theater types conducted a ritual of repristination lead by Rev. Raines. A thousand years ago on the Feast of Fools, priests and nuns would dance lewdly in the sanctuary and defile the altar, then on the morrow, All Saints Day, reverently cleanse and restore. Something of that sort was going on at Steamboat Methodist.

The play was being mounted during the second year of a very bad economy. And as Dracula was rehearsing, the snow wasn't falling. Businesses which had been teetering began to tumble. Each morning another one would be gone, another "out of business" sign. It was as if some night creature was stalking and killing the townsfolk. It didn't snow. And no visitors came to town. And so instead of swelling double and triple its size, which was normal in the winter, Steamboat shrank in upon itself. Steamboat Rep was counting on audiences who would never come.

By the last act the little community of the play had shrunk, too. Each new morning revealed some new horror. Lucy dead, Mina infected, Van Helsing wounded by the monster, and in one way or another the rest of the cast dispensed with, or put out of commission. In the end, a wobbly Mina, half minion to Dracula, led the way to the sepulcher with the stake, followed by old Van Helsing who, with a broken arm, could only carry the hammer.

Dracula lay on his bier, Mina placed the stake, and Van Helsing pounded it right into the chest. The sound was a whirlwind or a jet engine. It made you want to run. Frozen air in a foggy wave washed over the audience as the count screamed, music thundered, and blinding light came down through Michael's window whiting out the battleground. The audience stood. The play wasn't over, but they stood. One evening, several performances into the fun, something flew through the air and landed on the stage. A sock. Next night there was a rain of socks. The play, the audience said, knocked their socks off. It became a tradition during the curtain call.

Instead of empty houses, we were jammed. With no visitors in town the show sold out and was extended. After his giddiness settled, Richard became anxious. What had we done? He wanted to do it again, of course, with every show, for the rest of his life. What had happened?

Laurence Olivier, after an especially brilliant night, came raging backstage.

"Larry, old chap," someone said, "what's the matter? You gave the performance of a lifetime!"

"I know," Olivier growled, "but I don't know what I did!"

It felt like that. Was it the mythic form? The music? The stone people? The special effects? Of course, all that helped, but it wasn't enough to account for what we'd seen. We saw a community that ought to be depressed and anxious turn out each night to cheer and applaud.

Metaphor for Change

It took many years for Richard to figure it out. By that time, Steamboat was thriving, having decided after that terrible winter to pool their resources and install snow making equipment. What finally explained *Dracula* was a little book, *The Conscious Use of Metaphor In Outward Bound.* (Bacon, 1983)

According to author, Stephen Bacon, actions (like supporting other climbers by holding the rope "on belay") can be metaphorical for, say, pulling one's weight in a family. For an under-achieving youngster, being on belay brings about a crisis, which, if resolved in the Outward Bound experience, may change her life at home. What this hypothetical youth held wasn't simply a rope, it was an isomorph, says Bacon, an event with the same shape as another event, but without the mass and complexity. What the girl experienced in mind and muscle was that she could be depended on. Supporting the weight of fellow climbers, and carrying family responsibilities had, for the boy, the same psychological shape. The power of healing events like this one is that the participants don't recognize consciously what's going on. For the girl, it wasn't till later, when she was at home, that she realized her empowerment. (Bacon, 1983, p. 9)

Holding other youngsters on belay wasn't exactly the same as pulling her weight in her family. Nor was defeating Dracula the same as thing as overcoming economic downturn. In both cases the smaller event was similar, *but with important differences:*

- The performed event had far less "mass" than the life event, making it easier to create in the first place and easier to modify and repeat.
- The performed event allowed participants to rehearse—to repeat over and over—the steps of the ritual, until they were confident and comfortable with the process.
- In the performed event the actors experienced victory whereas in the parallel life event, they were experiencing defeat.

- Following the performed event it was possible, in both cases, to re-write the stories and create different and preferred real-world outcomes.

Steamboat Springs survived. The church got its social hall, and Harold wrote an editorial praising Steamboat Rep and calling the experience a miracle. But the true miracle may have been the breakthrough conversations following the play.

That dark winter, even as the shops were closing, people were talking. "What are we experiencing?" "What would it take to create change on this issue?" The answers were hard in coming, because they demanded that the community with a mashed thumb, so to speak, not just think about making the thumb feel better. Before it could heal, Steamboat needed to ask itself, "How are we already whole?" "Where is our future already showing up?" If their "What have we just experienced?" question brought nothing but pain, then the best they could hope for was short-sighted, quick-fix thinking.

During these conversations, did Dracula cross anyone's mind? It is certainly an answer to "What have we just experienced?" As in the play, contending and disparate parts of the Steamboat community banded together for mutual preservation. Not many years before, Steamboat Springs had been a small town with one restaurant at the foot of the ski mountain, and a single rope tow ski lift. Now the town was a welter of competing interests, interests that all saw the issue differently, each with its own agenda.

The miracle was, despite major obstacles—private and public corporations, city, county and state governments, contending egos, and conflicting constituencies—Steamboat finally followed the pattern of Mina, Seward, Harker and Van Helsing. That winter was the last time the empty sky would threaten the community. They pooled their money and resources and bought and installed snow making equipment.

Dracula was years behind Richard when we made this realization. *Dracula* didn't cause the town to band together, but it was part of the change-making field that enveloped the little community which learned to save its own life: first through story, performance, relationship, and conversation, and finally through committed action. Steamboat crossed the Story Bridge.

Massive social change can move outward from the stories we tell and the conversations we have. Juanita tells the story of how a small group gathered at a friend's home, a young businessman, and began one of the largest movements in Germany since the end of World War II. Over steak and wine, the conversation turned to the skinhead attacks on foreign workers. Somewhere among the courses the group challenged itself to step outside the silent majority and do something. Their stories, their performances that night, deepened their relationship and their commitment to righting this injustice. Conversation led to action. By dessert each had agreed to contact others and bear witness to the injustice.

The first candlelight vigil drew one hundred people to a popular downtown bar. Each agreed to contact others for a second event. In short days the "candlelight conversations" spread. Churches, schools, businesses, and organizations stepped forward. The small group of friends and the nation were stunned when four hundred thousand people turned out for the Munich vigil.

Inspired by their Munich brethren, groups all over the nation moved spontaneously to conversations and their own vigils. Over five hundred thousand turned out in Hamburg, two hundred thousand in Berlin, and one hundred thousand more in Frankfurt, Nuremberg, and other cities. A national dialogue emerged on the acceptability of neo-Nazi behavior. In the light of a million flickering candles, Germany saw itself more clearly and turned firmly against the behavior. This story is all the more powerful since it took place before the present-day connectivity of cell phones and social media.

The Arab Spring began the same way. One person experiences an injustice and is moved passionately to tell the story. Other people, in the performance of witnessing, pull the story into a powerful shape. Their shared performance bonds them, and attaches them to their community and their cause. Stories evolve into conversations appreciating the full dimension of the situation. These divergent conversations and stories begin to strike lightning, ideas for action emerge and spontaneously are enacted.

It isn't one cycle, the process is fractal. It reiterates story/performance/relationship/ conversation/action again and again at every scale of magnitude. It is one person whispering in the ear of another whose head begins to nod. A few words are exchanged, and out the door they go to perform some action. It is tens of thousands in Tahrir Square, performing their stories, witnessing, building relationship and community, using the people's mic (shout a phrase, the crowd shouts it back with a thousand voices) to carry on mass conversations, shaping, harvesting ideas, and moving to action.

The pattern of the Story Bridge process is as ancient as people coming together for change. The difference between a violent revolution and manageable social change is the difference between an explosive and a fuel. When social temperatures soar, the process erupts spontaneously with explosive intensity and violence. Intentionally deployed, before the boiling point is reached, the Story Bridge could fuel the crossing to wise and considered action. In the explosion, hideous stories create the human fireball. Crossing the Story Bridge provides heat and energy that melds people, ignites conversations, and starts heartbeats and footsteps toward action.

Saying Yes To New Ideas and Change

Decades ago, the stores in Steamboat were going out of business. People were out of work, and wondering what was going to happen. More recently, the economy took a turn for the worse. Jobs were not to be had and neither were the grants that once funded the work of Community Performance.

Instead of waiting for things to get worse, or for *Dracula* to be slain, we set about to shift our organization. We could no longer work as we had. We had to change. But we didn't focus on the problem, "How can we get the resources to do our brand of theater?" Instead we used our pro-active conversation question, "What is possible now that wasn't possible before?" We'd been collaborators *in the field* of Community Performance. Now we became radical collaborators *in the evolution* of Community Performance.

When Community Performance began, we were out in front of the *zeitgeist* and so our innovation was incomprehensible to many. When we'd talk, for instance, to a banker about supporting the project that would become Swamp Gravy, when we'd explain that diverse people pooling and performing their stories would change the psychology and the economy of the little town, the banker looked at us like red-haired step children. Over a generation, we've watched Community Performance grow into a phenomenon, become the next best thing, then lose some of its luster. Where once Swamp Gravy was sold out a year in advance, now one could get a ticket even on the night of performance. It wasn't that the shows weren't as good; in fact they were better. But they were no longer the cutting edge; the newness had worn off.

In Europe a millennium ago, people of letters were rare and very special. Possessed of a magical skill, they were called "grammarous." Centuries later, when most people could read and write, the word split into two meanings. "Grammarous" continued for a time to refer to people of letters, then died out. But the word's other referent, to enchantment and charisma, remained useful; one of its sounds shifted, and the word we know today was born, "glamorous." Community performance may have passed the glamorous phase, but a second phase is upon us- the phase we are morphing toward. In the next phase, story performance and conversation leadership become part of the ordinary life of the community. At a planning weekend in Abbeville, Louisiana we could hear that idea being expressed by a community leader.

> *This is an experience and a process that should continue in the community. It should become a movement. Will Allumé (lead organization) sponsor these (story/conversation workshops) every month and across the ethnicities? This process is inspiring and hopeful. It brings a community together. This process should...[be] an ongoing function.*

As we move in this direction, the story-to-change process is attracting allied groups that increase community development outcomes: community gardens, time banks, schools, long-term care facilities, and places of worship. Projects and Partnerships like these make future communities stronger.

What's Possible Now? The Co-evolution of Humans and Story

Stories and humans are able to define a new era of co-evolution. In it, we utilize story as we always have, but, in addition, we utilize story with intention. We can have a great Café conversation to listen in on how story intertwines with, enriches and challenges the human experience. And from those stories, those divergent conversations, the clouds of possibility would charge with what is to be next between humans and story. What is to be next in this grand relationship?

We watched Maxine and Tammy make a similar realization on the first day at the Rowan Community, the Medicaid nursing home that has been transformed into the lived experience that might be titled "I Am Home." Rowan had put into practice "relationship," "person-centered care," and "quality circles." Staff had "cross-trained," "modeled," and "role played," going so far as becoming residents for extended periods to garner that experience. They were already using story performance and just didn't realize it.

But by recognizing they are living *in* story, and tapping into the wisdom that has grown up around story and performance, they might readily, and perhaps radically, improve their process. A "learning circle," where people describe problems and brainstorm ways to solve the problem, might, Maxine suggests, be replaced by a "Story Circle Café." Instead of going after the problem of accidentally mixing up residents' drugs, and trying to figure out how to fix the problem with protocols and procedures, one might hold a story circle. "Tell about medication experiences that inspire you..." Creating a hospitable and safe space, encouraging deep appreciation, might bring you to stories and conversations about people living drug free with dementia, for instance. You can't mix up pills you don't hand out. Realizing we're living in story, story which can move naturally into conversation, starts to make all kinds of insights happen.

Lightning Strikes

Divergent conversations charge the cloud of possibility, and often prompt lighting strikes. In Steamboat, lightning stuck in the form of snow making equipment. With the Yarn Exchange, Aiken First Presbyterian Church, and Staging Change Institute attendees, lightning is striking in a number of ways.

The last pier in the bridge comes when conversations provide questions that lead to committed action:

What key learning, insight, or discoveries am I taking with me?

How are they relevant to my own life at home or work?

What is possible now that wasn't possible before?

What specific seeds of possibility am I taking?

Where will I plant these seeds?

What specific action steps will I take to plant these seeds and how will I nurture them?

Divergent conversations, which open up ideas and possibilities, lead to lightning strikes as those ideas converge into action plans. In the short time since discovering the need for conversation and committed action, the energy from our Community Performances as well as workshops have created more than a dozen different actions, with sustainability in mind, in different areas of the community, well outside of the doors of the theater.

- Jules and composer/musician Brett, are creating stories of downtown Jonesborough buildings, Storytown. People can hear the stories by reading code badges with their smart phones. It's a way for the walls of Tennessee's oldest town to tell its stories.
- Harlan County, Kentucky has received an ArtPlace grant by the National Endowment for the Arts. With them we will be using the story-to-change process as a way to develop locations and activities for youth around the arts and especially music and theater. They are geographically spread out and are trying to imagine what performance, music, and story look like spread across their many small towns and hamlets. The story-to-change process with its power to energize and focus toward action may be a tool to focus their collective wisdom.
- With the Jonesborough Yarn Exchange company, we created Story of the Carols, a sing-along Christmas carol event including a narrative by Jules of stories (local, historical, and traditional) associated with each carol. The project enabled JYE to create an easy event of community service and fellowship. The cast and town loved it, and it's become popular on our website and will be

available to other communities at Christmas. Already a Valentine's version of sing-along is in process.

- Ed has been taking his growing story wisdom along with his JYE friends into every corner of life. From the pulpit Ed's insights interpret bible verses in the light of his experience of the Story Bridge. Conversation about community didn't start with JYE, but Ed's orientation has changed markedly: "You can argue with opinions and be divided by them. You can share stories and be united by them."

- In Abbeville, Louisiana a weekend CPI workshop of stories and conversation has brought the town's great strengths into focus and inspired people to develop a play at the same time they're listening in on their future through critical conversation bringing together their diverse populations.

- With the Jonesborough Yarn Exchange and other storytellers CPI has developed a monthly show, in the style of an old fashioned radio show, using local stories, regional music and comedy skits based on life in Jonesborough. We have partnered with ETSU's broadcast department, and are working out a plan to broadcast the performance on the air.

- A partnership is developing between CPI and leaders in the field of congregate senior living. The idea is simple. In ways big and small use the Story Bridge to engage seniors with each other, their families, and their surrounding community. The ultimate purpose in senior living is to actively connect individuals and help them create a collective sense of place and community – an empowered culture of active purpose and participation both within senior living and in the community at large. Activities range from resident-created albums of picture and story for each new arrival which build relationships and turn strangers into friends, to monthly radio show stage performances that bring the talents, people, organizations, music, and stories of the seniors to the community, and the community to them.

The Story Bridge itself is the result of a "Why don't we..." lightning strike. Several of the Institute attendees are realizing wider applications for the bridge. Simultaneous explorations are beginning in several states and in widening fields of interest. This book is one.

One attendee in Aiken, South Carolina utilized the Bridge to celebrate the culmination of twenty years of pastoral leadership in her church and to take the topic of the church's positive future into critical conversation.

The Rowan Community (a Medicaid nursing home) and the Colorado Culture Change Coalition, both part of the nationwide Culture Change movement in long-term and elder care, are partnering with CPI to develop the Bridge as a support of their movement. Radio shows, modeled after the ones in Jonesborough, are beginning at Rowan. The aims of Culture Change and the story-to-change process overlay and inform one another.

We haven't struggled to make these. The process is self-organizing. The "we" is the organism; organismic self-regulation is the rule. When the group moves through the steps of the bridge, it arrives inevitably at the other side. But the fractal nature of the process means that new stories, performances, relationships, conversations, and actions are happening all the time. They flow into the bridge from every direction. It's no surprise that the things we listen to, focus on, are grateful for, notice with most careful attention, manifest.

Margaret Wheatley, author of many books on systems thinking and the tendency of all living systems to self-organize, says:

> *Today, with the possibility of more conversations, including electronic ones, we are witnessing in magnified form what Margaret Mead described many years ago, the power of small groups of committed people to change the world. In a new understanding of how large change originates, researchers are finding that these changes begin in small ways, in conversations among friends — at kitchen tables, tenement stoops, cafés, town plazas. From that willingness to join together in conversation, small plans are born, local actions taken. As they ripple out through webs of relations, others learn of our efforts and join with us. Larger actions take form and global impact becomes visible. There is no power equal to the power of a community conversing with itself about what it wants. Meaningful conversations create the power to change, create or transform institutions, values, and worldviews ... We are now living with this global information network that supports millions of conversations ... In a networked world, size doesn't matter. Meaning matters. Small localized activities that have meaning for others quickly span the globe. It is critical connections, not critical mass that's important... Through processes of seeding the conversations, consciously connecting and linking the conversations together, feeding back*

information and insights into the network, we seek to catalyze this worldwide web into a global leadership presence whose strength and intelligence is far greater and richer than the sum of its parts. (Brown, The World Café: Living Knowledge Through Conversations That Matter Dissertation, 2001, pp. 191-192)

EPILOGUE: A STORY WORTH LIVING

Story, shared in community, offers believable, meaningful, emotional proof of a deep truth: when things integrate, their optimal functionality is revealed. Story integrates people, events, and places into a meaningful whole. Fully to integrate the heart into the body is to connect it to every artery, vein, and capillary, enabling it perfectly to perform. The story-to-change process, from strangers to change-makers, encourages this quality of relationship. When each person in the group feels safe, free, and charged with enthusiasm to share in fullness her full self while the others deeply listen, and ditto for everyone else, then we are in a perfect circulatory system and every heartbeat affects everything everywhere.

We leave you with a few questions, hoping they prompt further stories, conversations, or self-reflections. *We love stories.* What if the anecdotal results of more than twenty years of fieldwork in communities and the research results around story and conversation are true? What if human groups "wake up," and come to consciousness and attention when their members begin to share stories? What if the collective human organism is only able to speak through the mouths of its people, their stories, and their conversations? What if story and conversation, intentionally applied, multiply many fold human intelligence and compassion?

If this were true, we would be welcoming a new species to the world—"We"—to create with love and joy on behalf of every "I." If this were true, what could you do—in your family, place of worship, community, and business—to bring this possibility within reach? What is the smallest increment of change you could take to test the hypothesis for yourself? What stories could you cause to be shared, exchanged, hefted and experienced?   What conversation could come out of that? What action?

Our organizations, communities, and corporations teem with examples of the remarkable integration of diverse elements.   We can choose to listen reverently to these proleptic and holographic stories, put them in our bodies and move with them till they are our own, grow relationships with the people out there moving with us toward our shared future, talk it over with them, go deeper, really interrogate the experience from the vantage of every different person, and then speak those future stories, and let the lightning come, let it strike, let the "What if we..." illuminations spark us to new actions, to new and positive futures.

Is that a story worth living?

About the Authors

Richard Geer's productions won awards and broke attendance records before he left the professional stage in pursuit of the question: Why theater? For more than twenty years, starting with Swamp Gravy in Colquitt, Georgia, Geer has stalked this collective art form to its roots in people, place, and story. He has facilitated scores of communities and organizations in their quest for deeper understanding. When people, place, and story coincide, wisdom appears that can be accessed no other way. Theater thus made is a collective way of knowing about the things that matter, that bind us together. Richard has been married for forty years to his sweetheart, Adrienne; they have three grown children and four grandchildren. Richard, and colleagues, continue to explore with communities and organizations. richgeer@aol.com

Jules Corriere has written thirty-eight plays, edited a book of oral histories, and recently completed a season writing and directing a monthly radio-variety show. Her production of Scrap Mettle SOUL's The Whole World Gets Well won the Presidential Points of Light Award and toured in London and Edinburgh. Other playwright credits include "Let My People Go! A Spiritual Journey" which performed at the Kennedy Center Concert Hall; and Turn the Wash Pot Down in Union, SC, featured in People Magazine and named by the state legislature as the First Official Folk Life Play of the state. American Theatre magazine said of this play, "Even if Turn the Washpot Down doesn't save Union 's life, it has already saved its soul." She appears in the 2010-2011 edition of Who's Who for her work in the field on Theater Arts and Social Activism. jcorriere@aol.com

Melissa Block is the Executive Director of Community Performance International. She has an MA in Practical Anthropology and believes that story-performance work is the most effective use of individual and community resources to craft a shared cultural identity. Melissa has worked in nonprofit community development for the last two decades, and is also the owner of Artist's Ally Professional Arts Management. cpidirector@post.com

Juanita Brown, Ph.D. is a co-founder of the World Café and co-author of the award-winning World Café book. Juanita is a thinking partner for senior leaders across sectors in creating innovative forums for strategic dialogue on critical business and societal issues. She was also a senior affiliate with the MIT Center for Organizational Learning.

David Isaacs is co-founder of the World Café, and co-author of the award-winning World Café book. David works with clients and colleagues in consciously designing, convening, & hosting powerful conversations around their most important questions. He has been a collaborator and coach with innovative learning programs in the University of Texas Business School Executive MBA program, CIIS, and KaosPilots University.

The People of the Jonesborough Yarn Exchange
During 2010, Jonesborough residents and community members shared their stories and memories of Tennessee's oldest Town. In 2011, they saw those stories come to life on

stage in an epic performance by the same community members. I AM HOME, under the umbrella title of Jonesborough Yarn Exchange, was performed by community members at the McKinney Center at the Booker T. Washington School in Jonesborough as part of the Mary B. Martin Program for the Arts, as well as during the International Storytelling Festival. In 2012, the Yarn Exchange members continue their story-performance work with A NIGHT AT THE YARN EXCHANGE, a monthly radio show that focuses each performance on new issue or segment of the community.

References

Bacon, S. (1983). *The Conscious Use of Metaphor in Outward Bound.* Denver, CO: Colorado Outward Bound School.

Brown, J. (2001). The World Café: Living Knowledge Through Conversations That Matter Dissertation. Pegasus.

Brown, J., & Isaacs, D. (2005). *The World Cafe: Shaping Our Futures Through Conversations That Matter.* San Francisco, CA: Berrett-Koehler Publishers.

Burnham, L. F. (2003, March/April). A More Perfect Union. *American Theatre.*

Kaufman, G. D. (2004). *In the Beginning-- Creativity .* Augsburg Fortress Publishers.

Prechtel, M. (2005). *The Disobedience of the Daughter of the Sun.* Berkeley,California: North Atlantic Books.

Vogt, E. E., Brown, J., & Isaacs, D. (2003). *The Art of Powerful Questions: Catalyzing Insight, Innovation, and Action.* Mill Valley, CA: Whole Systems Associates.

INDEX

S

T

W

Made in the USA
Charleston, SC
17 November 2012